walks in the secret kingdom
North Northumberland

Edward Baker

Published by Sigma Leisure – an imprint of
Sigma Press, 1 South Oak Lane, Wilmslow, Cheshire SK9 6AR, England.

British Library Cataloguing in Publication Data
A CIP record for this book is available from the British Library.

ISBN: 1-85058-623-3

Typesetting and Design by: Sigma Press, Wilmslow, Cheshire.

Cover photograph: the College Valley, looking north *(Edward Baker)*

Photographs: Edward Baker

Maps: Jeremy Semmens

Printed by: MFP Design and Print

fOREWORD

by Lord Joicey
Ford & Etal Estates, Berwick-upon-Tweed

I warmly welcome the publication of this book of walks for the Secret Kingdom – an area that is surely a paradise for walkers. Edward Baker is to be congratulated on compiling such an impressive collection of routes that will surely appeal to all ages and all abilities. I hope that Mr Baker's enthusiasm will encourage more people to appreciate the landscape, history and wildlife of this wild and beautiful land where some of us are so fortunate to live. As a local man, he clearly knows his patch and he has managed to choose a range of walks that represent north Northumberland in all its aspects. It is also pleasing to see that, as a family man, he has recognised the need for walks that can be tackled by the youngest of walkers; even toddlers will be able to tackle his short routes of two miles or so, but there are many more walks for the more adventurous. That, of course, is the attraction of country walking: children begin with family walks on gentle terrain and then graduate to tougher days in the hills.

Relatively few walkers seem to have discovered our part of England, and perhaps that is the appeal for some. But I believe that we must not guard this secret too closely: north Northumberland covers a vast area and there is more than enough space, with hundreds of miles of public footpaths, so that you can walk all day and never see another walker. And yet, when you walk into our villages or the local public houses, you will be assured of a warm welcome.

Nowadays, walkers and those who earn their living in the countryside – including farmers, farmworkers, forestry people and even those who run the local shops and pubs – must all co-operate to achieve their goals. As a local landowner, I must try to maintain our heritage for the enjoyment of future generations while ensuring that local farmers and other country people can prosper. Tourism is important to us – it brings additional valuable income to local businesses and helps to keep alive such scarce resources as public transport and the village pub. Walkers, being environmentally-aware folk, are particularly welcome and they can help to preserve the magic of our Secret Kingdom by acting responsibly (as the vast majority do). It goes without saying that you should follow the Country Code and obey the dictum of "leave only footprints, take only photographs" but you can go a little further by becoming involved in countryside issues and sharing the everyday problems and issues that face country people today. If you, as a walker, meet a farmer or other local person, be sure to greet him or her and have a chat – you may be surprised by how much you have in common. Discuss your shared problems – admire the beauty of the country-side – share your knowledge. Enjoyment and responsibility go hand-in-hand.

So – welcome to north Northumberland: admire our fine scenery, discover the magic of the Secret Kingdom and enjoy the splendid walks in this excellent guidebook.

Joicey

Contents

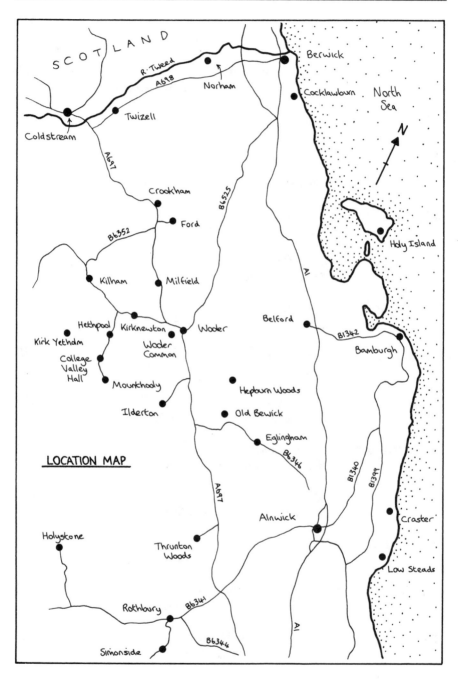

LOCATION MAP

entering the secret kingdom

Walks in the Secret Kingdom is a collection of walks within North Northumberland. For the purpose of this book the area referred to as North Northumberland covers the land between the River Coquet to the south and the Scottish border to the north. The western and eastern boundaries are the Simonside and Cheviot Hills to the west, and the North Sea to the east.

We will travel over diverse landscapes – rough moors, rolling hills, verdant countryside and dramatic coastal plains – giving endless options to the walker. Each walk reflects the character of the area, giving an insight into its history, wildlife and landscape.

History of the Kingdom

Man first appeared in this area around 3000BC. These Neolithic people were hunter-gatherers making use of the fish and berries which were available around the vast Milfield Lake. With the arrival of the Beaker people, Northumberland was brought into the Bronze Age. Around 800BC, Celtic invaders moved the area into the Iron Age. Huge forts were built, first on the plains and then on the hills. Grain crops became the main source of food although hunting and fishing were still important.

Christianity appeared briefly at first, dying out during the Roman occupation when Northumberland reverted to paganism. In AD596 Christian preachers came, and by the 7th century Northumberland had become a seat of Christian culture and learning under St Aidan at Lindisfarne. The 8th century saw the land pillaged and plundered by the Vikings, although later many settled and became farmers.

The Norman invasion of Northumberland was around 1069. Many castles were built to consolidate their position, and numerous churches were built around the same time.

Over the next centuries the area suffered badly from Scottish raids, with a continual state of war existing between England and Scotland. This lasted until the 18th century when the repercussions of the 1745 rebellion finally ended hostilities. After the end of the border skirmishes, the new stability allowed growth and peace to finally come to the land.

The Kingdom Today

Agriculture is now the main industry of North Northumberland. For a time the fishing industry flourished, but those days are now all but over. Only a small remnant of the original fleets still fish these waters, mainly concentrating on shellfish – the quality of which gives a better financial return. Tourism is a growing industry, but quiet roads, uncrowded beaches and countryside still predominate.

The coastline of north Northumberland between Amble and Berwick upon Tweed has been designated as an Area of Outstanding Natural Beauty. The stretch between Amble and Dunstanburgh is dramatic, with rocky outcrops and rugged cliffs. From Dunstanburgh northwards, wide, clean beaches and golden sand dunes are the rule.

At Bamburgh a mighty castle dominates the skyline. In AD547 King Ida built his royal capital here. Later, in AD993, the town was completely destroyed by the Vikings and did not recover till Norman times. In the graveyard at Bamburgh stands a monument dedicated to local heroine Grace Darling. In 1838, Grace, aged 22, assisted her father, the keeper of Longstone lighthouse on the Farne Islands. One stormy night in that year, the steamer *SS Forfarshire* was blown on to the rocks a mile away. Grace and her father rowed out in treacherous seas to rescue passengers from the doomed vessel. The story gripped the imagination of the romantic Victorians and Grace soon became very famous. The story goes that she was not happy about this and scorned publicity, being a shy and reclusive person. She died four years later from tuberculosis.

A short distance north of Bamburgh lies Budle Bay, a vast expanse of sand and mud flats. It is a world famous bird reserve, extremely rich in migrating sea birds and waders. The sandy beaches continue as far as Berwick upon Tweed, the northernmost town in England. Situated at the mouth of the River Tweed, the town was once an important port. It suffered badly during the Anglo-Scottish skirmishes on account of its location, between England and Scotland. It changed hands at least thirteen times before finally opting to become English. The harbour at Berwick is the home of one of the largest colonies of mute swans in Britain. A beautiful sight on a warm summer's evening.

Berwick hosts a colourful market twice weekly on Wednesdays and Saturdays. The town has an excellent museum at Berwick Barracks. It holds regimental memorabilia, a local history collection, and the Burrell Collection. The Berwick Walls are perhaps the best example of Elizabethan walls and ramparts still surviving, and can be completely circumnavigated on foot.

A large range of refreshments to suit every taste is available in Berwick. As a sweet treat, try some of the famous Berwick Cockles. Not a seafood, but a type of boiled sweet available locally.

Cautionary Notes

Clothing and Weather

The countryside of north Northumberland is very beautiful, but it can be remote and lonely in places. For those following the walks within this book I would strongly advise they prepare well before starting out. Wear clothing suitable for the (often changeable) weather conditions and the severity of the walk.

A walker who is unprepared is a danger to himself. In winter, extra clothing and some food are essential. Even the shortest walk could bring on fatigue and hypothermia. In summer, be sure to carry adequate drink and wear light clothing. A careless walker could end up suffering from heat stroke. Comfort and suitability of footwear are much more important than brand names.

Navigation

For ease of navigation, the walking instructions in this book are separated from background material. This is particularly important if night is falling and you need to return quickly to base:

✎ Walking instructions are set in this style of text.

Background material is inset from the margin in this contrasting typeface.

A sketch map is provided for each walk, but this is not intended as a replacement for the appropriate Ordnance Survey map, details of which are provided. An OS map shows details of the terrain and enables you to relate the route to the surrounding countryside. Remember to take with you the appropriate map plus a compass. If you do not know how to use a compass in conjunction with a map then please take the time to learn. It could save your life one day.

Grading

Distance and grades are given for all walks. The time to allow for a particular walk will depend on the terrain, personal fitness and the size of your group. A lone walker on level ground will easily manage 3mph, whereas a family group with young children may struggle to achieve half of this speed, thus doubling the estimated time for the walk.

Rights of Way

Most of the walks within this book are on public rights of way which are open to the public at all times. However, some use permissive paths or tracks. These are used at the discretion of the landowner and can be closed at any time. Please ensure that when you are on these permissive ways you use them carefully and considerately.

Dogs

If taking a dog with you, please ensure it is kept under control at all times and on a lead where advised. Some walks in this book cross grouse moor and the ground-nesting birds are easily disturbed, especially during the breeding season which lasts from May to June. Dogs must always be kept on a lead near sheep during the lambing season. A pregnant ewe can abort if frightened by a strange dog.

1. Bamburgh to Budle Bay

Distance: 4½ miles, 7.25km

Grade: Easy

Maps: Ordnance Survey Landranger 75, Pathfinder 465 NU13/23

Refreshments: There are pubs, hotels and cafés in Bamburgh.

Start: Car park off the main coastal road, opposite Bamburgh Castle. GR 183349

The walk begins in a car park below the mighty fortress of Bamburgh Castle before traversing the cliff top and shoreline to Budle Bay. Here there is a famous bird and wild fowl reserve and feeding ground for arctic migrants, waders and gulls from the breeding colonies on the Farne Islands. The walk returns via country lanes and agricultural paths. Bamburgh dates from the middle of the 6th century, when it was the royal city of King Ida, ruler of the ancient kingdom of Bernica. Today it is a quiet village clustered around a small, wooded green. Bamburgh is popular, its clean beaches a magnet for families. Sand dunes stretch north and south along this coast, which is justly famous for its wild, rugged beauty as well as its history and bird life.

✤ Leave the car park and cross the main coastal road. Turn left along the side of the road to the entrance drive leading to Bamburgh Castle. Cross the drive and go through a gap in the railings opposite. Continue along a path below the castle with the local bowling green to your left. The path exits on to a narrow, surfaced road. Turn right and follow the road as it runs parallel to the sea. Pass by a lighthouse on your right before reaching the entrance to Bamburgh Golf Club after a row of cottages.

Bamburgh Castle dominates the village and is visible from miles away. Since the 6th century the site has been fortified with structures of one sort or another. King Ida built the first fortifications when Bamburgh was a royal city. The Vikings raided and destroyed later fortifications. The present keep dates from the end of the Norman period. During the War of the Roses the castle was a Lancastrian stronghold. Attacked and bombarded with artillery, it was reduced to a ruinous state. Between 1894 and 1905 the castle underwent extensive renovations under Lord

Bamburgh Castle

Armstrong, a Victorian inventor and industrialist. Today the castle is still in the care of the Armstrong family.

✎ At the golf club is a signpost for Budle Point, directing you through wooden gates and over a broad, grassy path. Small, blue-painted wooden stakes guide you across part of the golf course. Just before reaching a stone wall, a blue stake off to the right points you to a lesser path, which takes you along the cliff top. After curving around Budle Point, the path proceeds along the side of Budle Bay before descending to a concrete gun emplacement, a remnant from the Second World War. Pass by the emplacement and follow the path as it drops to the beach and goes along the lower edge of a caravan park. Cross sand dunes to the single row of Heather Cottages, which will be to your left.

To the right of the end cottage is an English Nature National Nature Reserve notice board welcoming you to Lindisfarne.

✎ Pass to the right of the end cottage and on to sand dunes. There is no clear path from this point. Make your way by the best route available across the dunes, keeping Budle Bay to your right and the bank of the cliff to your left. Budle Bay is a shallow estuary that fills with sea water at high tide. After 100

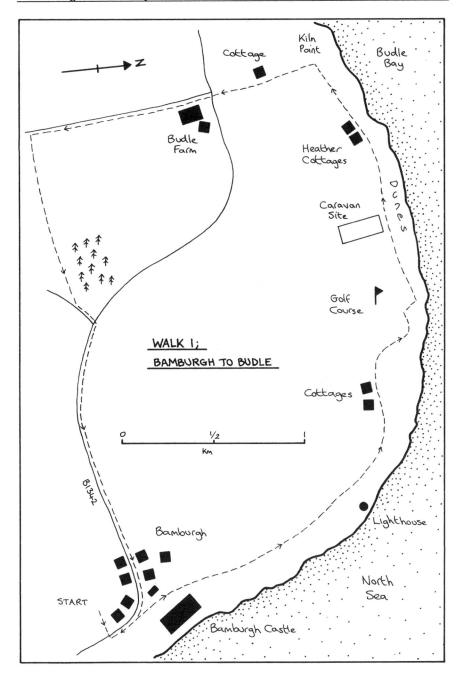

metres you come to Kiln Point, where a narrow lane leads inland from the dunes.

The nature reserve at Budle Bay is internationally important for wintering and breeding waterfowl and shore birds. Birds such as the pale-bellied Brent geese travel from the Arctic to feed on the beds of eelgrass in the winter. Eelgrass is one of the few higher plants that can grow in the sea below the tidal low water mark. The sand dunes and salt marsh contain a wide variety of plants and insects. In summer, for example, sea pink, marsh hellebore and many butterflies are seen.

↳ Take the lane from the dunes, passing through a gate to the left of cottages and continuing to join a public road. Cross the road and continue on a minor surfaced road to the right of the buildings of Budle Farm. Remain on this road for 800 metres to reach a signpost on your left bearing directions for Bamburgh. The signpost is some 75 metres prior to a road coming in from the right. Cross into the field using stone steps in the wall. The path travels along the edge of a field and parallel to a hedge on your right.

Field scabious grows in the hedge between June and October. The small, blue-petalled flowers have heads resembling pincushions.

↳ At the other end of this field the path dips to a stile on your right. Cross the stile and proceed, as indicated by a yellow arrow, along the side of a row of trees to another stile.

These trees are the remnants of an old hawthorn hedge, which has been neglected and allowed to grow wild over the years.

↳ Once across the stile the path contours the hillside below a stand of trees to your left. Beware of a well-defined, but incorrect path, angling off to the right. Where the trees end, bear half right towards a hedge across pastureland. Make your way to a gap in the hedge that holds a stile. Cross the stile and turn left along a minor road to meet up with the main coastal road to Bamburgh. Turn right and follow the road as it descends to the village and the start of the walk.

The church on your left as you enter Bamburgh is that of St Aidan. A wooden chapel used by St Aidan first occupied the site in the 7th century. The present church, built during the reign of Henry II, is a fine example of Early English architecture. An unusual feature of the church is a low, side window. This allowed those infected with the plague to receive communion. In the graveyard can be seen the tomb of local heroine Grace Darling.

Local Attractions

Bamburgh Castle is open to the public. A tour around the inside of the castle takes you through magnificent halls, reception rooms, the bake house, a Victorian scullery, the armoury and the dungeon. In the old laundry building can be found the Armstrong Museum. This contains many fine examples of industrial and aviation engineering. Light refreshments and drinks are available in the Clock Tower Tea Rooms. Enquiries and opening times – 01668 214515.

The Grace Darling Museum contains many relics and letters relating to this famous local heroine and her rescue of the passengers of the *SS Forfarshire* in 1838. The vessel went aground on the Farne Islands and Grace, the daughter of the lighthouse keeper, rowed out with her father despite the atrocious conditions to rescue passengers and crew. This deed established her name in history. She died four years later from TB, at the early age of 26, despite taking a rest cure at Wooler. Admission to the museum is free, although donations are appreciated. Enquiries and opening times – 01668 214465.

2. Belford to St Cuthbert's Cave

Distance: 9½ miles, 15km
Grade: Medium
Maps: Ordnance Survey Landranger 75, Pathfinders 464 NU03 and 465 NU13/23
Refreshments: Belford has a pub and a hotel.
Start: Belford – street parking.

This walk travels over agricultural land from Belford to St Cuthbert's Cave. The cave is traditionally reputed to be one of the resting places for the body of St Cuthbert, on its long journey from Lindisfarne to its final resting place at Durham in the 8th century. The monks feared frequent Viking raids on their monastery at Lindisfarne, and regarded the mother church at Durham to be a safer alternative for their beloved spiritual leader. The name Belford is believed to have derived from Beals Ford. The Blue Bell Inn in the centre of Belford dates back to the 18th century, when this was a stopping off place for the stagecoach between Newcastle and Edinburgh. Here the horses were changed and passengers could obtain refreshments at the inn. The first coach to pass through Belford was in 1786 and the last on July 5, 1847. Belford was once famous as a foxhunting centre and many of the characters created by Robert Smith Surtees, a well-known sporting journalist, were said to reside in the area. Next to the church of St Mary is Belford Information Centre. It is well worth a visit for background information on Belford and the surrounding area. In the 18th century Belford held a charter for a weekly market, as well as two busy annual fairs. The market has long since disappeared, but the fair has been revived as an annual carnival. The village streets are decorated with bunting and various community activities take place. Like the market, the castle that once stood in Belford has also long since disappeared. Belford West Hill Farm now occupies the site.

✎ From the village square, proceed up West Street. Turn right immediately after Belford Community Centre, as indicated by a public footpath sign, and go along a narrow lane taking you out of the village. Some 200 metres down the lane, at a point where it bends sharply right, is a signpost to your left bearing directions for Swinhoe. Pass through a kissing gate sited next to the signpost. A narrow path takes you to a gate in a wooden fence. Go through the gate and continue on the path. A wire fence will be to your right.

The castellated building across the fields to your right stands on the site of the former 'castrum de Beleford'. This castle is mentioned in the local records of 1415. Today this is West Hall Farm. A castellated building was a fortified house having turrets and battlements like a castle. It is possible that a wooden fort could have occupied the site as early as 1050.

❧ Go through the next gate and turn right along a path that keeps to the field margin. On reaching a small footbridge, cross over and proceed towards the right flank of a small hill ahead. When you come to the stone wall that encircles the hill, cross via a stone step stile to your right. Once over, continue to a marker post and keep ahead as directed, through gorse bushes, to the next marker post. Here you leave the main path and take a lesser path leading off to the left. Climb a slight slope and walk on to a marker post located to the left of an old stone wall. At the post turn right and keep parallel to the wall. The path rises through gorse to a fence corner. At this point turn to the right and walk along the side of a plantation.

In the latter part of the above section you have some good seaward views to your right. On a clear day you can see Bamburgh Castle, Holy Island and the Farne Islands.

❧ On coming to a fence across the path, cross using the ladder stile provided and walk on with trees to your left. Soon the buildings of Swinhoe Farm appear ahead. At the end of the trees cross the next ladder stile and turn half left. Cross pastureland, aiming towards a gate leading into Swinhoe Farm.

Please show consideration and make sure dogs are on a close lead and avoid disturbances whilst on the farm premises.

❧ Cross a ladder stile at the side of the gate and pass the farm buildings to a surfaced road. Cross the road and turn left to a signpost. Take the narrow lane to the right of the signpost, which leads to a wood. On entering the wood remain on a broad dirt track as it winds through the trees to a gate allowing you to exit.

The woods and the lake are private property. There is no public access into the trees and walkers should keep to the track as it is the only right of way.

✎ On leaving the wood, the path skirts a high rock escarpment dotted with gorse and rabbit holes. When you reach a gate in a wire fence, cross, using a stile next to the gate. Walk on a few paces to meet a broad farm track. Turn left and follow the track to a plantation.

The track forms part of St Cuthbert's Way, a new long-distance footpath of 100 kilometres running between Melrose and Holy Island. Leaflets giving more information on the walk are available from Tourist Information Offices within Northumberland.

✎ At the plantation, pass through a gate and enter the trees. After a few paces the track divides. The right fork is the continuation of St Cuthbert's Way, but we take the track to the left. On reaching a gate across the way, pass through. Keep to the track as it descends slightly and curves to the right.

Above and to your right are the sandstone outcrops of Raven Crags.

✎ The next gate you encounter allows you to leave the plantation. A broad, grassy path takes you onwards with a stone wall to your right. The path descends towards Holborn Farm ahead.

This area is where the monks of Lindisfarne had peat-cutting rights.

✎ On reaching a point where a stone wall comes in from your right, turn left and climb, following beside the wall to a gate. Go through the gate and turn left on a path taking you to the right of the large lake of Holborn Moss. The path then angles right, taking you away from the lake, and climbs gently. At a fork take the path to the right and ascend the slope of Greensheen Hill. Walk along the summit of the ridge to a white Ordnance Survey column.

From beside the column you have some superb views. To the west, the land stretches far away to the horizon, encompassing the Cheviots. To the east, the North Sea coastline dominates the scene.

✎ Pass by the Ordnance Survey column and descend with the path over heather to the plantation seen ahead. At the plantation turn right and walk beside the trees to a stile. Cross the stile and take care as the path now makes a steep descent At the foot of the descent, the hollow of St Cuthbert's Cave is to your right.

The cave is reputed to be one of the resting places of the body of St Cuthbert on its long, convoluted journey from Holy Island to Durham in the 8th century. On the walls of the cave, humorous visitors over the centuries have carved their initials with dates and messages. Many of these are very old, dating from the early 1800s, whilst others recall poignant memories of lovers from the last war.

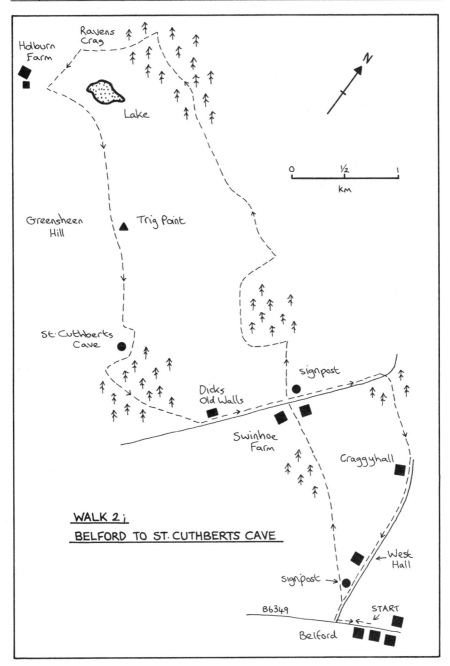

WALK 2;
BELFORD TO ST. CUTHBERTS CAVE

St Cuthbert's cave

✤ Take a path leading down from the cave, and at the foot of the descent turn left, along the edge of the trees. At a fence across the path, cross using a stile to the left of the gate. The path continues around the edge of the trees before coming to a gate that allows you to exit the plantation. Follow a broad track with a stone wall to your right. The wall is later replaced by a wire fence. Pass to the left of a small plantation and to the right of the next one. The track takes you past some stone buildings, which are known as Old Dicks Walls. Ahead of you are the buildings of Swinhow Farm. When you reach the signpost you passed earlier in the walk, continue ahead on a surfaced road. Where the road bends sharply left, you leave the road and take a rough forest track to your right. A signpost here bears directions to Craggyhall and Belford.

When walking these woods in 1997 work was underway on harvesting the trees. Please take care here, as in any working wood, when felling operations are taking place.

✤ Proceed along the forest track, through the trees to a signpost. Turn right and on to a fork. Take the lesser path to the right, which will take you to a gate allowing you to leave the trees. Once through the gate, turn half left along the side of a field and parallel to a rock escarpment on your left.

The escarpment is Sunnyside Crags and is part of the Great Whine Sill, an extrusion of igneous rock. The sill stretches from the Farne Islands and through Bamburgh and Dunstanburgh. It also forms the base of Hadrian's Wall in west Northumberland, and continues on to Teesdale and the North Pennines.

↳ At a wire fence which crosses the path, cross via the stile to the left of a gate. Remain on the path until you reach the wide, iron gate leading into Craggyhall Farm.

To the left of the iron gate stands the well-preserved ruin of an old limekiln. Lime generated in this kiln was used as a fertiliser or as an antiseptic additive to lime wash for the local farm buildings.

↳ Pass through the gate and the farm buildings to a surfaced road. Keep to the road to arrive at West Hall Farm. Here the road bends left and then right as you pass through the farm. Remain on the road to return to your starting point.

Local Attractions

Belford Craft Gallery is well worth a visit. It stocks a wide selection of local hand-made crafts as well as an interesting collection of books and gifts.

3. Berwick Town Ramparts Circular

Distance: 2½ miles, 4km

Grade: Easy

Maps: Ordnance Survey Landranger 75, Pathfinder 438 NT95/NU05

Refreshments: Berwick provides a wide variety of cafés, restaurants, pubs and hotels to cater for all tastes.

Start: Pay and display car park next to Somerfields supermarket. GR998532

This historical walk takes you around perhaps the finest example of Elizabethan ramparts in Europe. Designed by Sir Richard Lee in 1558, the ramparts followed an Italian style of defence. The walls were built of earth and backed with stones. Protruding bastions defended the walls, and because they protruded they were able to provide covering fire for each other. The Elizabethan ramparts run from Scotsgate to Kings Mount, where they join up with the old medieval and Georgian walls of the town.

❧ From the car park, turn left and go through the stone arches of Scotsgate. Once through, immediately turn left up a short flight of stone steps. Take the next flight of steps to your left, set in a grass slope, to reach the top of the walls. Turn right at the top and walk along the surfaced path. The car park is below to your left as you walk on to Cumberland Bastion.

Originally named Middle Mount, it later changed to Cumberland Bastion after the Duke of Cumberland passed through Berwick on his way to the infamous Battle of Flodden in 1746. The battle devastated almost a whole generation of Scottish nobility.

❧ From the bastion, keep to the path and away from the edge to your left. Pedestrians have been known to fall from here. Ahead of you is Brass Bastion.

Brass Bastion owes its name to a brass cannon once sited there. For a time the bastion was known as Search House Bastion because of the guardroom located there for the benefit of the search watch that patrolled the walls. An interesting local tale tells that if you walk around the bastion three times at midnight then Satan will appear before you. I would not chance it. It could be true and I would rather put off that experience for as long as possible.

The Brass Bastion

✤ From the bastion, again rejoin the surfaced path as it heads south to pass Holy Trinity Church on your right. Built around 1650, the church replaced an earlier medieval one. Just after the church you cross over the Cowgate entrance built in the walls.

The stone arch of the Cowgate entrance dates from 1595. It was through this gate the people of the town drove their cattle to and from the fields.

✤ Immediately after Cowgate, the imposing 18th-century stone buildings of Berwick Barracks are to your right. They house a fine military museum as well as an interesting town museum. Looking left, across the green area known as The Fields, the North Sea can be seen. Continue along the path to reach Windmill Mount.

Windmill Mount is named after a windmill that occupied the site in 1587. During the Second World War there was an anti-aircraft battery positioned here.

✤ After walking along another stretch of wall you pass by a flight of steps leading down into the walls. Look to the left and you will see King's Mount.

King's Mount was first named St Nicholas's Mount, taking its name from the church that once occupied the site. Later the name changed to

Hudson's Mount after the Earl of Hudson. He was the governor of Berwick from 1568 till 1587. Later still, around 1603, it was renamed as King's Mount.

↳ The path descends quaintly named Kipper Hill to arrive at Fisher's Port. As you make this decent the town allotments are on your right.

Fisher's Port was built in 1522 as a gun battery and overlooks the mouth of the River Tweed. The single black cannon, which is on display, was captured in the Crimea and later presented to the town.

↳ From the Port, walk on a short distance to Coxon's Tower, a former lookout post.

A narrow flight of stone steps takes you to the top of the tower where you have an excellent view overlooking the Tweed estuary.

↳ After Coxon's Tower the path bends right and runs inland, following the bank of the Tweed. The fine restored houses to your right date from the 19th century. Below to your left is the quayside. After the row of houses you will notice a single-storey stone building to the right. This was the main guardroom.

The guardhouse dates from the 18th century and was originally located at Maygate in the town. In 1815 it moved, brick by brick, to its present site. The building was renovated by English Heritage and the interior restored by Berwick upon Tweed Civic Society for used as a heritage centre. It houses an exhibition depicting the history of the town, its walls and port. The centre is open to the public during the summer months.

↳ The path passes along the Quay Walls, where the houses date from the 17th century. Of particular interest is number thirteen. This building was the customs excise house from 1825 till 1917. The walk continues on to the end of Berwick Bridge.

Berwick Bridge is one of three bridges spanning the Tweed. Built between 1611 and 1634, it replaced earlier wooden ones. The earliest recorded was in 1153. Looking further upstream is the Royal Tweed Bridge. Built for road traffic, the bridge was opened in 1928. Further upstream is the Royal Border Bridge, which opened in 1850. This magnificent iron bridge carries the main intercity rail link between London and Edinburgh.

↳ Cross the road and walk along the bank of the river and down Bridge Terrace, with its interesting collection of 18th-century houses. When you come to the fork, take the pathway to the right that climbs a slope taking you under

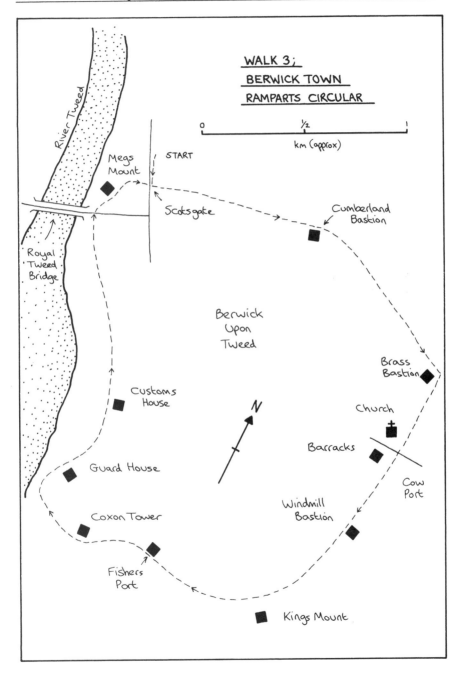

WALK 3;
BERWICK TOWN
RAMPARTS CIRCULAR

0   ½   1
km (approx)

River Tweed

Megs Mount

START

Scotsgate

Cumberland Bastion

Royal Tweed Bridge

Berwick Upon Tweed

Brass Bastion

Customs House

Church

N

Barracks

Guard House

Cow Port

Windmill Bastion

Coxon Tower

Fishers Port

Kings Mount

the Royal Tweed Bridge. At the top of the slope, and to your left, you pass the statue of Lady Jenningham.

Lady Jenningham died in 1902. Her husband, Sir Hubert Jenningham, late Member of Parliament for the borough, presented the statue to the town.

↳ Passing the statue, the path curves right and through a narrow, iron gate before turning left to Meg's Mount.

Meg's Mount, built in 1558, owes its name to a cannon nicknamed Roaring Meg that once stood here.

↳ From Meg's Mount the path crosses over the Scotsgate. This was built in 1590 and so-named because it was the entrance to the town from Scotland. Descend the steps to your right and then turn right again to descend another flight of steps. At the foot of the steps turn right to return to the car park and your starting point.

Local Attractions

Berwick Barracks contain the Borough Museum and Art Gallery, the Regimental Museum of the King's Own Scottish Borderers and the William Burrell Collection. Enquiries and opening times, telephone 01289 304493.

4. cocklawBuRn naTuRe ReseRve

Distance: 1½miles, 2.5km
Grade: Easy
Maps: Ordnance Survey Landranger 75, Pathfinder 452 NU04/14
Refreshments: Berwick Upon Tweed (3½ miles) has numerous pubs, hotels and cafés.
Start: At the parking area at the south end of the coastal road. GR032481

A gentle stroll to explore a coastal nature reserve with a return journey along part of the shoreline of this heritage coast. Cocklawburn is about three and a half miles south of Berwick upon Tweed. The reserve comprises dunes with rich lime soils. Lime kilns once proliferated in this area. Many rare flowers may be seen in season, such as cowslips and orchids. There is also an abundance of butterflies and moths that feed on these lime-loving plants. The reserve, owned by the University of Newcastle, is open to the public. Obviously all flora and fauna are strictly protected and picking of flowers is forbidden. Look out for fossils and bird life on the seashore.

Go through the gap in the wire fence at the south side of the parking area. Next to the gap is a signpost proclaiming Cocklawburn Nature Reserve. A well-defined path crosses meadowland for thirty metres to a fork – take the right-hand path. Keep a low, grass-covered ridge to your right. On top of the ridge stands a concrete Second World War bunker. When you come to the next fork, take the path to the left to a stile set in a wire fence.

During your walk you will see a wealth of wild plants growing in the meadowland on both sides of the path. Depending on the season, you may see birds trefoil, bloody cranesbill, purple vetch, lady's bedstraw, knapweed, ragwort and meadowsweet. Many butterflies are attracted to the area with its abundance of food plants. For example, you may see the small blue, tortoiseshell, meadow brown, burnet moth and cinnabar moth.

Cross the stile, taking a path to the right. The one to the left goes to the beach and is the one by which you will be returning. The path travels next to a fence to a gate. Go through the gate.

The plants found on this stretch include wild thyme and rosebay willow

Lime kilns, Cocklawburn nature reserve

in the summer. In spring, cowslip and primrose enhance the area with their delicate beauty.

✎ The path climbs a gentle rise to join a broad dirt track. Ignore a lesser path leading off to the left and walk on, parallel to a wire fence on your right. When you come to a broad, grassy path leading off to the left, leave the dirt track and follow the path to a wire fence and a stile. Do not cross this stile, turn right and walk along the side of the fence to the next stile. This is where you cross over the fence. A path leads between two large sand dunes and onto the seashore.

There is a notice board beside the sand dunes warning that the dunes along the beach are unstable and dangerous. It is wise to follow this advice. There have been fatalities amongst the shifting sands of the dunes. A young boy was killed when the tunnel he had dug collapsed, suffocating him. If you have children with you, please keep an eye on them.

✎ Turn left along the beach towards a small headland where you will have to negotiate a rocky section to reach the next bay.

The rocky slabs at the headland, with their bubbled appearance, are the result of rapid cooling of lava flows when the landscape formed millions of years ago. A colourful assortment of pebbles is found on the beach.

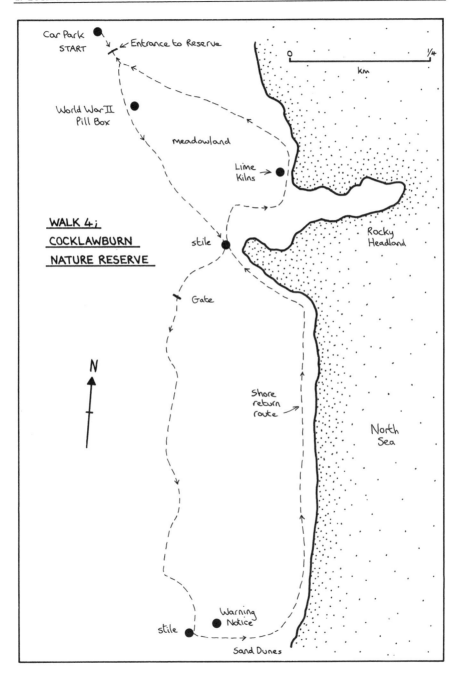

Car Park
START

Entrance to Reserve

km

World War II
Pill Box

meadowland

Lime
Kilns

WALK 4;
COCKLAWBURN
NATURE RESERVE

stile

Rocky
Headland

Gate

N

Shore
return
route

North
Sea

Warning
Notice

stile

Sand Dunes

When polished they can be used as decorative jewellery. After heavy storms stranded jellyfish often litter the beach.

↳ After crossing the rocks, walk on towards the next headland. Just after reaching the rocks, a path at their base leads inland and off the beach. Follow this path as it climbs to a stile in a wire fence.

This particular path from the beach has suffered from coastal erosion, and in places the soft, crumbly cliff has totally collapsed. For your own safety, **do not venture too near the unstable cliff edge.** The shale at the base of this cliff is a good hunting ground for fossils, mainly brachiopods. These are the fossilised remains of primitive marine invertebrate animals, dating back millions of years. In rock pools along the beach you can find fossils of crinoids. They are locally known as Cuthbert's Beads because of their tubular bead-like appearance.

↳ At the top of the cliff, cross the stile. Turn right to follow a path beside the fence. After 50 metres the path angles to the left and away from the fence before crossing a shallow gully. When you reach another stile in a wire fence, do not cross. Turn left and walk on to meet a broad track. Cross the track and follow a narrow, grassy path adjoining the cliff edge.

Looking right, just below the top of the cliff, can be seen the ruins of a limekiln. This is one of the many that operated in the area during the 18th century. In those days lime was used both as a fertiliser and as a lime wash. Houses were lime washed annually as it was believed to have sterilising properties, combating diseases, lice and bed bugs.

↳ Keep to the path to return to your starting point.

Local Attractions

Berwick upon Tweed – see Walk 3, the Berwick Town Ramparts Circular.

5. college valley hall to commonburn

Distance: 7½ miles, 12km

Grade: Strenuous

Maps: Ordnance Survey Landranger 74, Pathfinder 475 NT82/92, Outdoor Leisure 16

Refreshments: Wooler (8½ miles) has cafés, pubs and hotels. Milfield (10 miles), on the A697 towards Cornhill, has the Milfield Country Café and Craft Shop.

Start: College Valley Hall. GR887252

A walk through forestry and over moor, calling at an abandoned farmstead. College Valley is private and owned by the Sir James Knott Charitable Trust. In order to preserve the beauty and tranquillity of the valley, only 12 cars a day are permitted beyond Hethpool. As the College Valley Hall is beyond this point, a permit will be required. These can be obtained from J. Sale and Partners, 18 Glendale Road, Wooler, and are issued free of charge.

୧ From the hall, follow a surfaced road signposted for Southernknowe and Goldscleugh. The road dips to cross a bridge spanning the College Burn before rising and passing to the left of Southerknowe farmstead. Go through a gate across the road and pass Coldburn and Dunsdale cottages. Keep the Lambden Burn to your right until you reach Dunsdale. Cross a bridge spanning the Lambden Burn and walk on, with the burn now to your left.

The walk follows the road for just over a mile up the Lambden Valley, passing under steep, towering crags, wooded hillsides and plantations.

୧ Just before reaching Goldscleugh, the road bends right to pass a bungalow. At the old farmhouse of Goldscleugh take a small path to the left of the poultry shed and cross the Lambden Burn by a narrow, wooden footbridge. Keep the burn to your right and follow a path to a wire fence. Cross via a stile and continue along a well-defined path to a wooden shed and a sheepfold.

Most sheepfolds are made with stone but this one is unusual in that it is entirely made with wood. Freshwater trout are often to be seen in the Lambden Burn. Unlike sea trout, they spend all their lives in freshwater streams and lakes.

↳ Pass through the gate in a wire fence across the path. Walk on for 200 metres to a path branching off to the left, which takes you up the steep slope of Coldburn Hill. Pass between the gateposts of a fence that no longer exists. The path levels to follow the contour of the hill.

Take care when on the path ascending Coldburn Hill. It has eroded in places and can be slippery after wet weather. Even more so if adorned with sheep droppings.

↳ On reaching the top corner of a coniferous plantation, pass through a gate in the wire fence to your left. Turn right and go along the top edge of the plantation.

Large areas of Northumberland are planted with coniferous trees. After the First World War Britain found itself desperately short of timber. The Forestry Commission was established to replenish the nation's forestry and provide enough timber to cover future needs.

↳ Pass through the next gate to enter an area of more recently planted trees before the path goes through a wicket of broom. Continue onwards down a broad firebreak between the trees.

Keep your eyes open on this stretch through the trees and you may see some of the roe deer and foxes that have their homes in this area. You may see the odd adder or two out basking in the sun on hot days. The adder hibernates from September to April. The mating season is around May and June, with the young born August to September. It takes four to five months for an adder to mature fully. They feed on frogs, mice, small and young birds. The adder is recognisable by the dark zigzag stripe down its back. Beware, this is a poisonous snake and bites require urgent treatment. Bites are rarely fatal to humans but can prove otherwise with dogs.

↳ On coming to a path leading off to the left, leave your path and follow this new path as it climbs through the trees to a gate. The gate allows you to exit from the plantation. Keep to a broad track leading from the gate. On reaching the stile in a wire fence to your right, cross over.

On clear days you can see the distant North Sea on the horizon to the east.

↳ Once over the stile, a path curves left and takes you across Broadstruther Burn before wending its way along the side of Broadhope Hill. After cresting a rise the ruins of Broadstruther Farm, sheltered by a stand of trees, will be

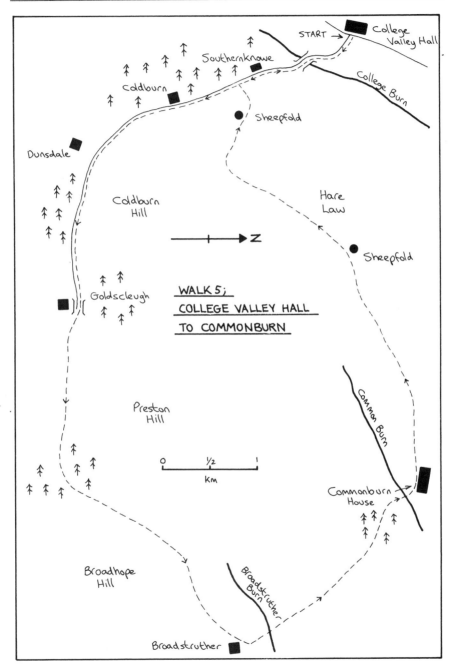

START → College Valley Hall

Southernknowe

College Burn

Coldburn

Sheepfold

Dunsdale

Coldburn Hill

Hare Law

Sheepfold

→ Z

Goldscleugh

WALK 5;
COLLEGE VALLEY HALL
TO COMMONBURN

Preston Hill

Common Burn

0   ½   1
km

Commonburn House

Broadhope Hill

Broadstruther Burn

Broadstruther

seen below you. The path descends to a gate in a wire fence. Go through the gate and cross rough grass to arrive at Broadstruther.

Broadstruther, now derelict and in ruins, was once a prosperous farm. The atmosphere of the place exudes peace and tranquillity. I often sit here listening to the silence and watching the wildlife pass by.

✎ Pass to the side of the ruins to a broad track. Turn left on to the track and follow as it descends to the Broadstruther Burn. Ford the burn and turn half right to a marker post bearing a yellow arrow. Turn left as indicated up the slope of a hill. Further marker posts guide you to the top. From the top you can see the buildings of Commonburn ahead. The path descends to a plantation entered by a stile. Keep to the path through the trees, and exit, using another stile, on to moorland.

The moors around Commonburn are managed for game bird shooting. Would walkers please make sure that if they have a dog it is on a lead at all times.

✎ Turn half left to cross the next stile and proceed to the banks of the Common Burn. Ford across and go up a short slope to pass along the side of the farm buildings.

Should the burn prove impossible to ford after heavy rain, there is a footbridge a short distance upstream.

✎ After passing the farm buildings, turn left and aim for a stile in the fence ahead. The stile is 250 metres to the right of a farm gate. Cross the stile and bear half left across a field to a gate in the wire fence opposite. Go through the gate and keep to the path as it contours the side of Newton Tors to your right. The path curves to the right and begins to climb the hill, gradually lessening in steepness.

Ahead of you is the elongated hump of Cheviot. This is the highest point in the Cheviots and gives its name to the range. Cheviot is also the highest summit in Northumberland.

✎ At a junction with paths leading off to the right and left, continue straight ahead. Pass to the left of Hare Law cairn – seen above and to your right. The path goes to the left of an old stone sheepfold, then bends slightly left to a wire fence and a stile. Next to the stile is a signpost. Cross the stile, taking the direction indicated for Southernknowe. Keep a wire fence to the left for 200 metres before crossing a second stile onto heather moor.

This land is carefully managed for the benefit of game birds. At intervals sections of the heather are burnt off to allow the growth of fresh, young heather. The grouse like to feed on the new growth, whilst the old growth provides nesting habitats.

✎ The wire fence, now to your right, is followed until you reach the field corner. Leave the fence at this point and walk half left across open moor. Pass by a marker post bearing a yellow arrow about 100 metres from the fence. The path bends right and then left before passing a sheepfold. Keep to the path as it descends to a surfaced road.

Take care on the descent as the going is steep in places and can be slippery after a spell of wet weather. You could arrive at the bottom quicker than you would have thought possible.

✎ Once on the road, turn right to return to your starting point.

Local Attractions

Mounthooly Bunkhouse offers overnight accommodation in a renovated farmhouse to walkers wishing to explore the area more thoroughly. Single walkers and groups of up to 25 can be provided for. Bookings and information from Mounthooly, College Valley, Wooler, NE71 6TX. Telephone 01668 216358, preferably evenings.

College Valley hounds

6. confluence of the Rivers till and tweed

Distance: 2½ miles, 4km

Grade: Easy

Maps: Ordnance Survey Landranger 74, Pathfinder 451 NT84/94

Refreshments: Tillmouth Park Hotel, about half a mile west on the A698 towards Cornhill. Salutation Inn, 3 miles east on the A698 towards Berwick. The Collingwood Arms, Cornhill − 3 miles. Coldstream (4 miles) has numerous pubs, hotels and cafés.

Start: Car parking area adjacent to Twizel Bridge. GR885433

This walk begins and ends at the old Twizel Bridge over the River Till. The bridge is famous for its connections with the Battle of Flodden in the 16th century. It is also justly appreciated for its architectural interest. There follows an excellent riverbank walk along two superb salmon fishing rivers, then past a fine example of a Victorian railway viaduct. The return on field paths leads to a romantic folly before descending through trees to the starting point. The wooded banks of the Till and Tweed are rich in wildlife, whilst the fishermen and gillies on the river seem caught in a time warp. A beautiful walk on a summer's day, although it can be equally appreciated in all seasons.

♭ From the parking area, go through a metal gate in the stone wall. There is a sign to the side of the gate requesting you to keep the entrance clear. Once through the gate take the left fork of the path. This takes you down a grassy, tree-lined path to the banks of the River Till.

Looking left along the riverbank you will see the single arch of Twizel Bridge. The Selby family built the bridge in the 16th century. It was over this bridge that the vanguard of English artillery, under the command of Admiral Thomas Howard, crossed the Till on their way to the Battle of Flodden. This enabled them to dominate the northern flank of the Scottish army of James IV, and contributed directly to the ultimate defeat of the Scots.

♭ Turn right to go along the riverbank and pass under towering crags to your right.

Perched on these crags is Twizel Castle, which you will have the opportunity of viewing more closely later in the walk. Giant hogweed infests the side of the riverbank. This plant can grow to a height of 12ft or more. Along the banks of the Till it is spreading in epidemic proportions. Attempts to eradicate it have had no success. Walkers should keep away from this plant as contact with it can cause painful blistering of the skin on exposure to sunlight.

↳ Continue on the pleasant path beside the riverbank and ignore a rough forest track leading off to the right. Soon the graceful arches of an impressive bridge come into view. Pass under the arch of this magnificent example of Victorian workmanship.

The bridge used to carry the old railway line running between Berwick and Kelso. The line opened in 1849. There used to be a station at Twizel, which opened in 1861. In 1955 it closed to passengers, and carried goods only until its final closure in 1962.

↳ Keep to the path as it winds through a patch of giant hogweed and then through trees to reach the junction of the two great salmon fishing rivers of Till and Tweed. A well-placed seat provides an ideal spot for a snack with the sight and sound of moorhens, ducks and swans to capture your interest.

Twizel Bridge, above the River Till

Across the Till to the left you will notice a ruined stone building. The early Lords of Tillmouth had a chapel here but it was neglected and allowed to fall into disrepair. In the 18th century Sir Francis Blake rebuilt the chapel and dedicated it to St Catherine.

↳ The path bends sharp right to travel along the bank of the River Tweed. On coming to a fence, cross over using the stile. To your right will be a cottage. Bear left when the path forks and keep parallel to the riverbank.

The River Tweed is internationally famous for its trout and salmon fishing. The Tweed is the longest river in the region. Its originates in the Tweedsmuir Hills, and it flows into the North Sea at Berwick. A distance of 95 miles.

↳ On reaching a point where there are some steep crags across the river, turn right, leaving the riverbank, and pass to the left of a small cottage. The path angles left to climb through trees to a road. Cross the road and pass a row of cottages. Once past the cottages the road widens and bends to the left. Some 250 metres down the road there is a signpost to your right bearing directions to Twizel Bridge. Cross into the field using the stile next to the signpost. Walk half left over pastureland to the impressive ruins of Twizel Castle.

Sir Francis Blake built Twizel Castle as a folly. Work on it began in 1770 but was never completed. A castle did originally stand here but was destroyed in 1496.

↳ Pass to the left of the castle, keeping parallel to a wire fence. At the stile cross over and turn left along a path with a wire fence on the left. The path soon bends right and descends through trees to return you to your starting point.

Local Attractions

Coldstream Museum displays military memorabilia and the history of the world-famous King's Own Scottish Borderers. Enquiries and opening times, telephone 01890 882630.

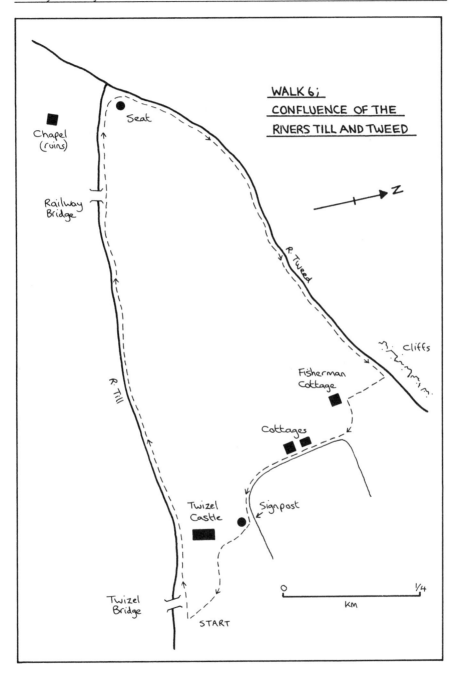

WALK 6;
CONFLUENCE OF THE
RIVERS TILL AND TWEED

7. CRASteR to ÖunStanBuRgh

Distance: 4½ miles, 7.25km

Grade: Medium

Maps: Ordnance Survey Landranger 75 and 81, Pathfinder 477 NU21/22

Refreshments: The Jolly Fisherman in Craster provides food and light refreshments. Adjoining the car park is The Bark Pots, a café and gift shop.

Start: National Trust car park at Craster. GR256197

This walk provides an interesting blend of coastal and country walking with the added attraction of a romantic ruined castle to visit before returning to Craster. Craster was once a thriving fishing village with its own herring fishing fleet, but sadly these days are over. Apart from a few fishing boats, it now caters to the tourist trade. The village is the home of the famous Craster kipper, renowned by gourmets worldwide. Kippers are herring cured by smoking slowly over oak chippings. Cured traditionally in this way they bear no resemblance in either taste or appearance to the dried fish available commercially. Craster has been a fishing haven from around 1626 and the harbour was built in 1906.

✤ From the car park, cross the main road and go through a gate in the stone wall ahead. To the right of the gate is a signpost bearing directions for Dunston Square. From here a well-defined path takes you through a planting of mixed native broad-leaved trees.

> The path is fringed with a variety of wild flowers. In summer the most common is the bloody cranesbill and the herb bennett. The cranesbill, a type of wild geranium, has violet blue flowers that are at their best between June and September. In the autumn the leaves turn dark red and look like splashes of blood, hence the name. Herb bennett has delicate yellow flowers between May and September and prefers to grow in damp woods and hedges.

✤ The path emerges from the trees to continue along the side of another group of trees to your right. On coming to a gate in a wire fence, pass through and walk parallel to a rocky escarpment on your right.

> The escarpment is part of the Whine Sill. This rocky ridge of dark quartz dolomite was formed 280 million years ago during volcanic activity,

when igneous rocks welled up between the largely carboniferous strata and much later lay exposed on the surface.

✎ Ignore a rough track leading off to your right. Go through the next gate and on a dozen paces to meet a farm track. Turn left and after negotiating another gate, walk along the side of a field towards the buildings of Dunston Square Farm visible ahead. At the top of the field go through the gate and turn right to follow a narrow, concrete-surfaced farm road. After crossing a cattle grid the road rises slightly to pass to the left of a small plantation.

To the left of the plantation stands a concrete pillbox, one of many found in the area. Erected during the Second World War, they formed a first line of defence against airborne enemies along this part of the coast. On the horizon to your left the distinctive whale-backed shape of Cheviot can be seen. To your right, peeping above the escarpment, the ruined towers of Dunstanbugh Castle are visible.

✎ The road continues towards Dunston Steads Farm. At the farm the concrete road becomes a farm track and passes through farm buildings and out onto a surfaced road. Turn right and walk to a gate at the end of the road. Pass through the gate to the green of a golf course.

This is Dunstanburgh Golf Course. To the left of the gate is a National Trust information board and a map of the area, including some alternative suggestions for the exploration of the coastal strip.

✎ Walk across the golf course to the sand dunes ahead. Just before reaching them, take a narrow path off to the right. This takes you up on to the dunes and to the left of another concrete pillbox. Ahead of you the ruins of Dunstanbugh Castle stand out against the skyline. Follow the path as it travels over the dunes.

Walking along the dune path you will encounter a variety of plants including knapweed, thrift, maidenhair and ragwort. Ragwort is a poisonous plant to mammals. The cinnabar moth takes advantage of this by laying its eggs on the leaves of this plant. When they hatch, the yellow- and black-striped caterpillars consume the leaves, absorbing the poison without harm to themselves. They are then rendered poisonous, so protecting themselves from being eaten by predators. Their brilliant colouring warns of danger to any bird looking for a tasty meal.

✎ This fine stretch of coastal path soon arrives at a wire fence and a gate. Beside the gate is a National Trust sign.

Looking half left, the stark cliffs of the Whine Sill rise 90ft upwards.

They are alive with a massive colony of gulls. During the breeding season the noise and smell are awesome.

↳ **Pass through the gate. The path curves around the base of Dunstanburgh Castle in a large semi-circle to the front entrance.**

The castle dates from 1316 and was built by Thomas, Earl of Lancaster. After the War of the Roses it was left to natural decay. Built on the Whine Sill, it occupies four hectares. On three sides it is defended by walls and towers; the fourth is protected by high cliffs and the sea. The castle has its own ghost, Sir Guy the Seeker. The story is that Sir Guy was travelling through the area when a storm forced him to seek shelter amidst the ruins. Falling asleep, he was later awoken by a wizard. The wizard beckoned him to follow and led him down a winding tunnel to a large cavern. Around the sides of the cavern lay sleeping knights. At the far end Sir Guy saw a beautiful maiden asleep in a crystal tomb guarded by two knight skeletons. One held a horn and the other a sword. Sir Guy immediately fell in love with the maiden. The wizard offered to set the maiden free if Sir Guy made the right choice in picking either the horn or the sword. After a long hesitation Sir Guy took the horn and blew a mighty blast. The sleeping knights awoke and the wizard jumped and laughed with glee. He tormented Sir Guy for making the wrong choice

Dunstanburgh Castle

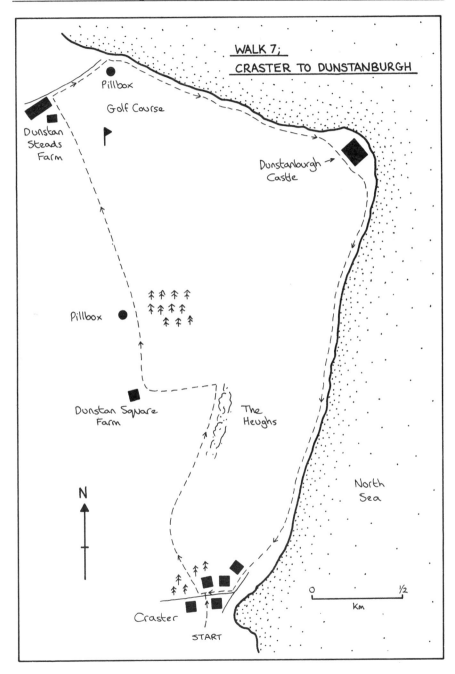

WALK 7;
CRASTER TO DUNSTANBURGH

Pillbox

Golf Course

Dunstan
Steads
Farm

Dunstanburgh
Castle

Pillbox

Dunstan Square
Farm

The
Heughs

North
Sea

N

Craster

START

0   ½
Km

and accused him of being a coward. Sir Guy sank to the floor senseless. He awoke in the morning to find himself lying in the ruined gateway. It is said that Sir Guy still roams the castle at night, seeking out his lost love.

↳ Turn right, away from the castle entrance, and follow the rough track of the castle approach road to a wire fence. Pass through the gate to a well-defined grassy path. This follows the coastline for about a mile to the fishing village of Craster. On entering Craster, pass the single row of houses before turning right up the main road to return to your starting point.

On this stretch of coastal path you will pass through a number of gates. Please take care to close these gates after you as livestock is grazed in this area right down to the beach.

Local Attractions

Dunstanburgh Castle's impressive ruins date from the 14th century. The castle itself comprises of a gatehouse/keep, two massive towers and a curtain wall enclosing four hectares. An admission fee is charged. Enquiries and opening times – 01665 576231.

8. cRasteR to howick

Distance: 4½ miles, 7.25km

Grade: Medium

Maps: Ordnance Survey Landranger 81, Pathfinder 477 NU21/22

Refreshments: In Craster there is the Jolly Fisherman pub and, adjoining the National Trust car park, the Bark Pots café which provides light refreshments. You could end your day in gourmet style by sampling delicious, locally-caught crab or traditional oak-smoked Craster kipper, a Northumbrian delicacy. Both are available in Craster.

Start: National Trust car park in Craster. GR256197

Another splendid walk combining countryside and coastal paths and with the option of a diversion to visit the beautiful gardens at Howick Hall. These are especially worth visiting for their spring displays and autumn colour. The walk then returns to Craster. The Craster family of nearby Howick Hall built the tiny harbour at Craster in 1906. It was dedicated to the memory of John Craster who was killed on active service in Tibet.

✤ From the car park, turn right towards the harbour. The road turns right to pass the lifeboat station and the Jolly Fisherman pub. At the end of the street turn right and then left to go along Heugh Street. Where the street ends, turn left and cross a playing field to a coastal path. Turn right along the path and follow as it takes you along the top of the cliff to a stile. Cross the stile and continue, with marker posts guiding your way. At Cullernose Point the path bends to the right.

Cullernose Point is a rocky headland and forms part of the Whine Sill. The cliffs have attracted large breeding colonies of gulls. The nooks and crannies of the rock face make ideal nesting niches for the seabirds.

✤ Descend to a gate, which you go through. A blackthorn-lined path takes you to a gate with a signpost bearing directions for the coastal path to Boulmer. Follow the coastal path through trees and dense undergrowth. Beyond the wall to your right is the main coastal road, which can be busy in summer. The path emerges on open ground and bears left away from the road to follow the coastline.

The whole coastline stretching from Amble in the south to Berwick upon Tweed in the north has been designated as an Area of Outstanding

Natural Beauty. Selected areas have been assigned as Sites Of Special Scientific Interest. Geologically, this stretch is very important, having many fine examples of rock strata and limestone folding. These are easily seen from the path.

♭ As you proceed along the cliff top a stone house becomes visible ahead. Pass to the right of the house. A strong stone wall protects the house on the seaward side.

The house was built in Victorian times for the Grey family and used as a bathing house. To the south of the house is a lovely, sheltered bay, ideal for a picnic or rest.

♭ After passing the house, bear right to a signpost next to a gate.

The signpost bears directions for the coastal path to Boulmer. Coastal erosion has made the path unusable. However, it is possible to walk along the beach to Boulmer at low tide.

♭ Go through a kissing gate to the side of the gate. Follow a grassy path for 200 metres to a gate leading on to the coastal road. Once through the gate continue along the road, heading away from the coast, to the entrance of Howick Hall.

Howick Hall was built in 1782 for the Grey family and has extensive gardens. These are open for public viewing. In spring the gardens are strewn with daffodils. Later in the year rhododendrons provide a blaze of colour.

♭ Turn right through the visitor's car park. Ignore a turning to the left. Leave the car park on a path running parallel to the side of a wood. After passing the wood continue along a field edge to a gate. Go through the gate and along the side of the next wood. At the end of the trees you will see a gate to the left bearing a public bridleway sign. Do not go through the gate. Walk on a dozen or so paces to another gate. Go through this gate and bear half left across a field towards the left edge of the rocky ridge ahead.

The ridge is Hips Heugh and is part of the Whine Sill. A heugh is an inland cliff or scarp.

♭ At a stone wall at the end of the field cross via the stile. There will be a signpost for Craster beside the stile. Bear half left and walk along the base of the ridge to a gate set in a stone wall. Go through the gate and along the edge of a field with a stone wall to your right. Soon the buildings of Craster South Farm will appear ahead. At the farm ignore the first turning to the right. Pass farm cottages and go through a gate. Turn right and walk down a track to the

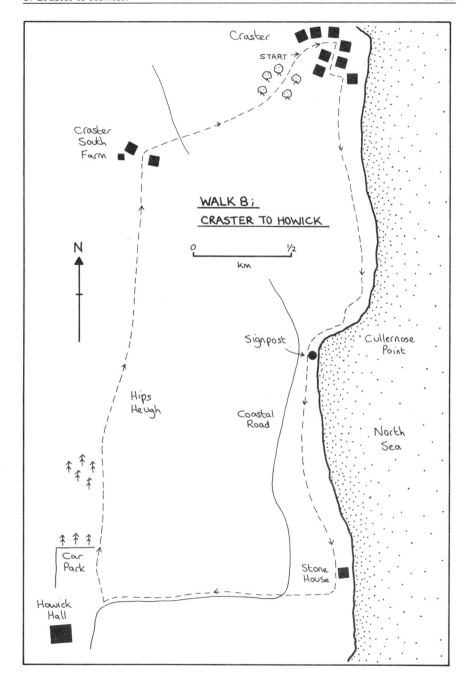

Craster

START

Craster South Farm

WALK 8;
CRASTER TO HOWICK

0   ½
km

N

Signpost

Cullernose Point

Hips Heugh

Coastal Road

North Sea

Car Park

Stone House

Howick Hall

coastal road. Cross the road and go through a gate in the stone wall. Cross rough pasture and enter a wood. Enjoy a pleasant stroll through the trees before emerging in the car park at the starting point of your walk.

Local Attractions

Howich Hall Gardens were largely designed by the 5th Earl and Countess Grey. They are aimed at garden lovers and kept free from commercial exploitation. From mid-April to the end of June, azaleas, rhododendrons and magnolias flourish in a sea of colour. From June to September, the herbaceous gardens come into prominence. In September the woodland garden is most attractive. To the northwest of the hall, a bog garden has been created. The gardens are open from early April to late October. An admission fee is charged. No dogs are allowed within the grounds. Car parking available. Enquiries and opening times, telephone 01665 577285.

Howick Hall

9. cRookham to floƆƆen

Distance: 7½ miles, 12 km
Grade: Medium
Maps: Ordnance Survey Landranger 75 and 74, Pathfinder 463 NT83/93
Refreshments: The Blue Bell Inn on the A697, at the Branxton turn off.
Start: At Crookham village. Park considerately on the roadside verge next to the public footpath signpost. GR917382

The Battle of Flodden took place on September 9th, 1513. It was fought between Scottish forces led by James IV of Scotland and English forces led by the Earl of Surrey. The battle began about 4pm, and by the time night had fallen many thousand lay dead and dying. Battle ceased with darkness and both sides retreated to lick their wounds. Next day the battle resumed. James IV was killed and the Scots were utterly routed. It was a terrible defeat for Scotland, with many Scottish families losing sire and son. This was the last great battle between the two countries.

✤ Turn left to leave the road as indicated by the public footpath signpost. Pass through a market garden on a path passing cottages before bending right to descend gently to a field. Keep near a fence to your left as you walk to a footbridge in the far left of the field. Cross Pallins Burn before turning left to go around the side of a small stand of conifers to the A697 road. Cross the road and turn right. Proceed for 25 metres to a signpost bearing directions for Blinkbonney and Flodden. Go through a gate next to the signpost and up the field margin, keeping a wire fence to your right. Pass through a gate at the end of this field. Follow a path along the left side of the trees above Crookham Dene. On coming to a fence, pass through the gate.

At this point you can see the picturesque ruins of Etal Castle and the slowly meandering River Till.

✤ Remain beside the trees to the next fence and go through a gate.

Looking across the countryside to your left, you can see Ford Castle amidst a cluster of trees. On the horizon are the Kyloe Hills.

✤ The path curves right to another gate. Go through this gate and follow a broad, hawthorn-lined track for just over a quarter of a mile to a surfaced road. The buildings to your right are the farm cottages of Blinkbonney Farm.

Looking towards Blinkbonny Farm

Blinkbonney farmhouse was built in the 1830s. An unusual feature of the farmhouse is that it is built entirely of sandstone, which would have had to be transported over a great distance. The farm labourers' cottages, however, are constructed from local stone quarried from the hills over-looking the farm.

✎ Cross the road to a signpost slightly to your right which bears directions for Flodden. Take the track, as indicated for Flodden, passing a row of derelict cottages. The track then takes you up the side of a field towards a wood on Flodden Hill. On reaching the wood, go through a gate and turn left through the trees.

A notice beside the gates states this is Flodden Hill Quarry Nature Reserve. It is managed by Northumberland Wildlife Trust. Walkers are requested to keep dogs on a lead at all times to protect the wildlife.

✎ After 150 metres pass by Sybil's Well.

Sybil's Well is built of stone and set in the exposed stony bank to the right of the track. Water trickles from a lion's mouth into a small basin. An inscription on the well reads, 'Drink weary pilgrims and stay, Rest by the well of Sybil Grey'.

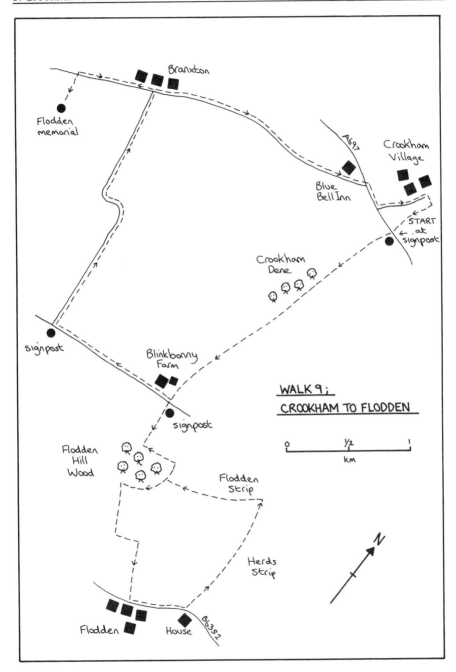

Branxton

Flodden
memorial

A697

Crookham
Village

Blue
Bell Inn

START
at
signpost

Crookham
Dene

signpost

Blinkbonny
Farm

WALK 9;

CROOKHAM TO FLODDEN

0   ½   1
              km

signpost

Flodden
Hill
Wood

Flodden
Strip

N

Herds
Strip

Flodden

B6352

House

↳ Continue along the woodland path, enjoying the wide views to the east. Wild flowers abound in spring, with snowdrops dominant in February. At a fork take the track to the right. Ignore a later track leading off to the right. The track then curves to the right and you will come to a marker post just before emerging on open land to your left. The post bears a blue arrow on a yellow background. Turn left down a grassy path to a gate. Go through the gate and along the side of a field with a wire fence to your right.

Looking straight ahead you will see the distant Cheviot Hill.

↳ At the bottom of the field turn left along the field margin. After 200 metres turn right and follow a track which leads towards Flodden Cottages. Turn left at the end of the field and go through a gate on to the B6352 road. Turn left again and follow the road for 450 metres to where it bends sharply to the right. There will be a house to your right. At this point turn left through a gate in a stone wall. A track leads along the side of a strip of trees called Herd's Strip to another strip of trees which crosses your path at right angles.

This strip of deciduous trees is called Flodden Strip.

↳ Once past a bend in the track, turn left and go along the strip to climb and re-enter the woods on Flodden Hill. Remain on the woodland track as it bends right to return you to the gate you passed through earlier, thus exiting the trees. Follow the broad track to a surfaced road where you turn left. After passing Blinkbonney Farm, continue along the road for about half a mile to a right turn. This will be signposted for Branxton. Follow this minor road as it ips and then rises up Branxton Hill ridge before finally descending into the village of Branxton.

Take a short break to explore and enjoy the Concrete Menagerie at Branxton. It is situated in a large garden to the right of the playing fields in front of you. The menagerie is collection of full-scale, hand-made concrete animals and birds. An information board explains the origin of the garden and its creator.

↳ Turn left and follow the signposts to the memorial commemorating the infamous Battle of Flodden sited just outside the village.

The memorial is a solitary stone cross. An information board to the side of the cross describes the battle and a map indicates the positions of the opposing armies. The memorial was erected by Berwickshire Naturalists Club in 1910. An inscription at the base of the cross reads 'Flodden 1513. To the brave of both nations'. A memorial service is held annually to commemorate the losses on both sides. A booklet explaining the battle is on sale at Branxton Church.

✎ Return to Branxton and continue along the road for a mile to emerge on the A697, next to the Blue Bell Inn, an ancient coaching inn. Cross the road and turn right before taking the next turning left to return to Crookham and the start of the walk.

Local Attractions

The Concrete Menagerie at Branxton is a wonderful garden filled with numerous life-size concrete models of wild animals. Admission is by donation and the garden is open at all reasonable times throughout the year.

10. ꝺoꝺꝺington to ꝺoꝺ law

Distance: 3½ miles, 5.6km

Grade: Easy

Maps: Ordnance Survey Landranger 75, Pathfinders 463 NT83/93 and 464 NU03

Refreshments: Available in Wooler (2½ miles), where you have a choice of cafés, pubs and hotels.

Start: Grass verge of road at Doddington, near to the telephone box. GR998324

The walk begins in the village of Doddington, climbs onto Doddington Moor and visits an ancient hill fort on Dod Law that commands fabulous views of the countryside. Littered over the moor are large rocks decorated with cup and ring marks. These were hand-carved by our Bronze Age ancestors.

In the 12th and 13th centuries, Doddington was far more prosperous, second only to Wooler. Its prosperity was based on stone quar-

"Cup and Ring" carved rock on Dod Law

rying, coal mining and agriculture. It is said that a church stood in Doddington before the Norman Conquest. One of the four wells serving the village was known as Cuddy Well after St Cuthbert. The original settlement was established by the Saxons around a freshwater spring known as Dod's Well. Today this spring runs out from the base of a large stone cross erected on the site in 1846. In 1584, to protect themselves against raids, the villagers built a bastle. The ruins can be found in the farmyard in the middle of the village. In 1826 a watchtower was built in the churchyard to guard against body snatchers.

✎ Proceed up the minor road signposted for Wooler Golf Club. Pass Cheviot View cottage on your right. On reaching a point where the road bends right to enter the golf club, there will be a public footpath signpost. Turn right, and a dozen paces on turn left along a grassy path. This joins up with a track that takes you to the closed entrance gate of a quarry.

Doddington red stone was extracted from this quarry.

✎ Turn left and cross a stile in the wire fence. Once over the stile, bear half left and follow a path through bracken. The path climbs gently at first then turns half left to cross a wide, shallow valley. This path may be indistinct when the bracken is in full foliage. Looking up left you will see the terraced ramparts of The Ringses. Keep to the path and on coming to a stone wall turn left. The Ringses fort lies before you. Take time to have a look around.

The Ringses is the site of a prehistoric hill fort. Three defensive ramparts of stone and earth encircle the fort to the south and to the east steep escarpments assured its position as a strong fort. Within the fort are traces of enclosures and hut circles.

✎ From the Ringses return to the stone wall and turn right. Continue parallel with the wall and head towards an isolated stand of trees ahead.

On maps this stand of trees is marked as Kitty's Plantation. Who Kitty was and how the name originated is unknown.

✎ Walk along the right-hand side of the trees. At the end bear half right to cross moorland to a wire fence. Cross a stile located twenty metres to the left of the gate. Turn half-right, as directed by a yellow marker arrow, and climb the gentle slope of Dod Law. At a fork take the path to the right and continue up the slope. At the top is another fork where you take the path to the left. This takes you to the summit of Dod Law.

On the summit, to your left stands an Ordnance Survey triangulation column. The column is within an ancient hill fort. The ramparts of the fort are clearly visible.

♭ The path descends to the right. To your right are the grounds of Wooler Golf Club. The green is one of the highest in the county. Two hundred metres along the path you should turn right and cross rough bracken to some flat stone slabs.

Cup and ring markings are carved on these slabs. These enigmatic marks were chiselled into the stone thousands of years ago. There are many theories as to their purpose, but no one knows for certain. To the north-west of the markings are the ramparts of an Iron Age hill fort.

♭ The path bends left and drops slightly to pass to the right of a cottage.

From this point the view overlooking Milfield Plain and the Cheviot Hills is tremendous.

♭ The path contours around the side of Dod Law, passing through dense bracken, and then descends steeply to a stile in a wire fence. Cross the stile. At the foot of the descent the path bends right through gorse bushes. At a fork take the lesser path to the left to pass down the side of a cottage and on to a surfaced road. Turn left to return to your starting point.

Finally, take an apple or a packet of mints with you on this walk as a gift for a famous Doddington resident, the Doddington donkey. He resides in the paddock next to the telephone box. He is grateful for all offerings from a flat palm and is loud in his thanks to one and all.

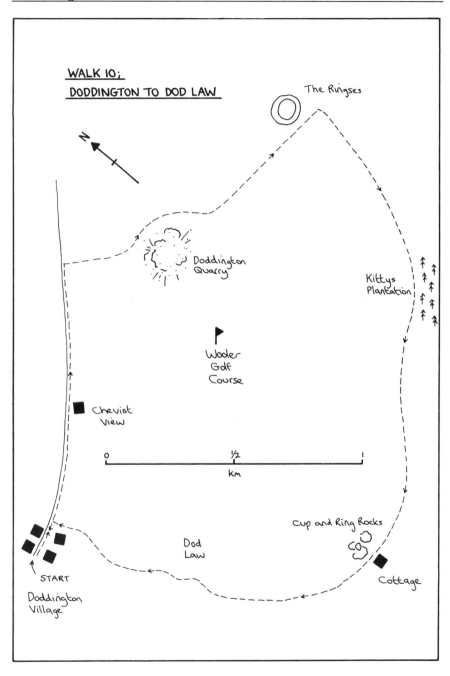

WALK 10;
DODDINGTON TO DOD LAW

The Ringses

N

Doddington
Quarry

Kittys
Plantation

Wooler
Golf
Course

Cheviot
View

0   ½   km

Cup and Ring Rocks

Dod
Law

Cottage

START

Doddington
Village

11. eglíngham to Beanly woods

Distance: 5½ miles, 8.6km

Grade: Easy

Maps: Ordnance Survey Landranger 81, Pathfinder 488 NU01/11

Refreshments: The Tankerville Arms, Eglingham

Start: Crossroads in Eglingham at the turn off for Beanly. Park carefully on grass verges of the B6346. GR105195

As this pleasant walk is rather short, it might be ideal for building up an appetite for lunch at the village pub. Alternatively, it could be used to work off the results of lunch. Eglingham is a pleasing village of stone-built houses straddling the B6346 Alnwick to Chatton road. The earliest mention of the village, then known as Eagwlfingham, dates back to the 8th century. It is thought the name denotes 'village of the church'. This could be a reference to the gift of the village to the monks of Lindisfarne in AD738 by King Ceolwulph. The church of St Maurice dates back to around 1200 and was built on the site of an even earlier one.

✎ At the crossroads, take the side road signposted for Beanly. Follow the road for almost a mile to a signpost to the left of the road. The signpost bears directions for Beanly and Titlington. Turn left, leaving the road, and cross a stile to the left of a metal gate. Follow a narrow path that angles half left away from the broad track from the metal gate. This path first takes you through gorse and then across bracken-covered ground towards the top of a small hill seen ahead.

The hill is marked on maps as The Ringses. This is the site of an ancient Celtic hill fort. There are three defensive ramparts of stone and earth surrounding the summit and these are clearly visible. Traces of hut circles have been found within the inner ring. A little distance to the west of the hill, several standing stones poke out through the bracken.

✎ The path travels through the centre of the hill fort and descends the slope on the other side. Continue through bracken for 400 metres then make a sharp turn to the right. Keep going through the bracken, heading for a low ridge seen ahead. Climb the ridge and cross level ground to a broad farm track. Cross the track and aim for the left corner of the plantation in front of you. At the corner is a gate allowing you access into the plantation.

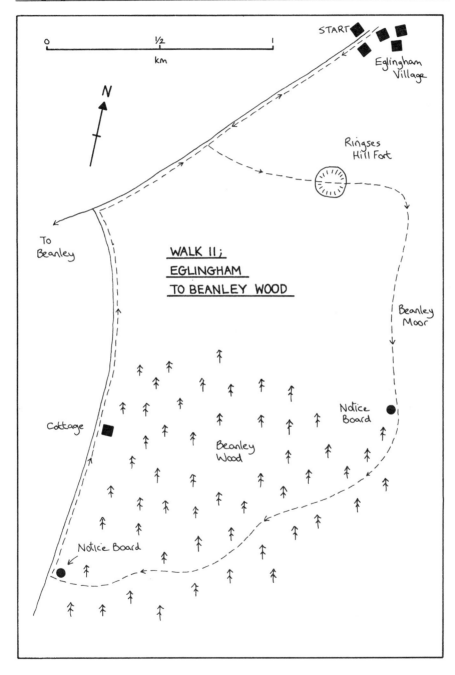

START

Eglingham
Village

Ringses
Hill Fort

To
Beanley

WALK 11;
EGLINGHAM
TO BEANLEY WOOD

Beanley
Moor

Notice
Board

Cottage

Beanley
Wood

Notice Board

N

0 ½ 1
km

To the left of the gate is a notice board, 'Border Consultants. Beanly Wood. Please take care. Do not start fires. In emergency dial 999. You are at Grid Reference NU104178.'

↳ Pass through a small gate to the right of the main gate and go along a broad forestry track.

The trees within Beanly Wood are mainly Scots pine and larch. Larch is the only coniferous tree that sheds its leaves in winter.

↳ The track winds through trees for just over half a mile before making a steep descent to a gate. This allows you to exit from the plantation.

To the side of the gate is a notice similar to the one you saw earlier when you entered the woods, except the Grid Reference is NU090172.

↳ A few paces on, the track joins a surfaced road. Turn right and follow the road as it takes you past Beanly Wood Cottage and along the side of the trees. The road joins up with another, where you turn right and continue along for one mile to return to your starting point.

Local Attractions

Alnwick Castle, situated in nearby Alnwick, is a large Border fortress dating from the 11th century. Restoration work was carried out in 1854 and 1865. The castle is the home of the Duke of Northumberland. The Abbots Tower houses the regimental museum of the Northumberland Fusiliers. Gift shop and tearooms. Enquiries and visiting times, telephone 01665 510777.

12. eglingham to titlington

Distance: 6 miles, 9.6km

Grade: Medium

Maps: Ordnance Survey Landranger 81, Pathfinder 488 NU01/11

Refreshments: The Tankerville Arms in Eglingham

Start: At the turn off for Beanly in Eglingham. Please park considerately on the grass verge of the B6346. GR105195

This walk combines farm roads, moorland paths and forest tracks. Eglingham once boasted two inns, but only one now remains. This inn, the Tankerville Arms, should not be confused with the inn of the same name in Wooler. The inn is thought to date back some 300 years. The village has many well-kept gardens and is particularly pretty in spring when rock plants cascade down the old stone buildings lining the main street.

✎ From your parking place, walk down the village main street, passing the attractive frontage of the Tankerville Arms on your right. Some 25 metres on, turn right and go along a lane to pass through farm buildings to a gate. Go through the gate and bear half left towards the top left corner of the field, where there is a stile in a wire fence. A few metres before the fence you must ford a narrow stream. Cross over the stile.

The ground around the stile can be boggy after adverse weather conditions so make sure that boots are securely laced.

✎ Keep to the right-hand side of the field towards a metal gate. Pass through the gate and then immediately through a second gate before turning left. Walk parallel to a fence on your left. Later, a stone wall replaces the fence before reverting back to a wire fence. At the point where the fence bends sharply left, leave the fence and walk straight ahead to ascend a slope to a gate set in a stone wall.

The area around this last gate was once the site of an ancient settlement. This is evident in the earthworks and hut circles visible on the ground.

✎ Pass through the gate and bear quarter right to climb a bracken-covered slope. Aim to pass to the left of a large boulder at the top. After passing the boulder, continue straight ahead across a wide, shallow basin overrun with bracken. Make your way towards the left of the escarpment ahead.

The path is indistinct and hard to follow at times due to dense bracken. However, as long as you keep aiming towards the left of the escarpment, you will not go wrong.

↳ On reaching the base of the escarpment, climb to the top. At the top, walk straight ahead through more bracken to a broad farm track.

Again the path is indistinct but just forge ahead until you encounter the farm track that is broad and well defined. To your right across the track can be seen Beanly Woods.

↳ Turn right along the track towards the corner of the trees, where another broad track leads to a gate allowing entry into the woods. Turn left and walk about halfway up this track before turning left to pass to the right of a large boulder. Continue through bracken, keeping three isolated conifers to your left until you reach new conifer plantings. Go through the plantings until you arrive at a stile in a wire fence.

Please note that these new plantings are not marked on present maps (1998).

↳ Cross the stile and follow a path ascending through heather over the small rise ahead to a wooden marker post. Continue ahead, as directed by marker posts, towards a broad farm track.

This section crosses shooting land. Please ensure that if you have a dog with you it is firmly on its lead at all times.

↳ Turn right on the track and remain on it, soon walking parallel to a fence coming in from the right. At the end of the fence there is a yellow marker arrow. Leave the track at this point, turning right to a gate leading into a plantation. Go through the gate and along a broad track cutting through the trees to a gate allowing you to exit from the plantation. Turn half left across pastureland to a gate located between a singe row of farm cottages and a large farmhouse to the right.

This is Titlington Mount, the halfway point of your walk.

↳ Go through the gate and down the side of the cottages to a farm track. Turn left and pass through a gate. Continue along the track and through the next gate. On reaching a further gate, bear half left along the left side of a plantation. After the plantation, cross moorland to a gate in a wire fence. Once through the gate cross rough moorland to a marker post. The path continues as directed to a gate in the wire fence ahead.

A sign next to the gate states that the land ahead is under a Countryside

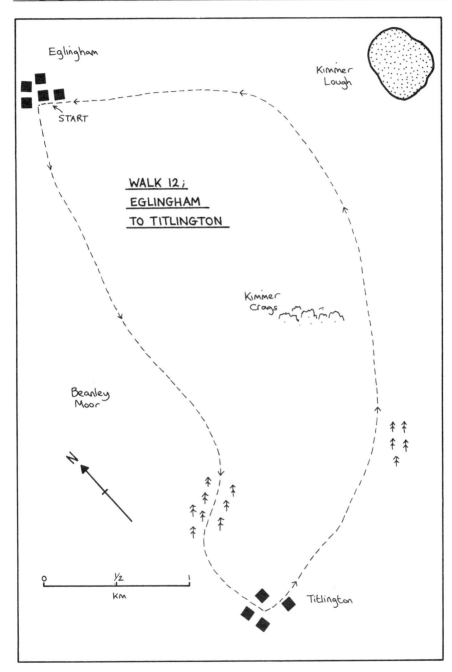

Eglingham

START

Kimmer
Lough

WALK 12;
EGLINGHAM
TO TITLINGTON

Kimmer
Crags

Beanley
Moor

N

0   ½   1
      km

Titlington

Stewardship. The occupier of the land allows free public access across the private fields or waymarked paths. This is part of a ten-year conservation plan under which the land is being managed. The public is welcome to walk and enjoy the countryside here until further notice. The owner of the land does not intend to dedicate any additional public rights of way over it. Existing public rights of way are not affected.

✎ Go through the gate and ahead to a marker post visible ahead. Pass by and on to the next post.

This post overlooks Kimmer Lough. This is a four-hectare (ten-acre) lake, stocked with fish and surrounded by reed banks noted for their wildlife.

✎ From the post, walk half left as directed by a blue arrow to the next post. The path then descends the hillside to a gate in a wire fence.

On the descent you can see ladder fern growing amidst the bracken. Later on the descent you will see heather, ling and sphagnum moss. Sphagnum moss was used to retain water in commercial flower arrangements and hanging baskets. It is a sure sign of wet land.

✎ Once through the gate, turn half left and cross a large field to a gate. Pass through the gate and walk along a field margin with a wire fence to your left. At the gate go through and follow a broad farm track. At the next gate ignore a turn to the right and go through the gate. Follow this broad track as it takes you to Eglingham Farm, where you turn right to reach the main street of Eglingham. Turn left to return to your starting point.

Local Attractions

See previous walk from Eglingham.

13. ꝼoꞃꝺ to ꞃoughtịng Lịnn

Distance: 6 miles, 9.5km

Grade: Medium

Maps: Ordnance Survey Landranger 75, Pathfinder 463 NT83/93

Refreshments: Etal (1 mile) has the Black Bull, Northumberland's only thatched pub. Real ale and excellent bar meals are served. Heatherslaw's Granary Tea Rooms (¾ mile) serve light refreshments and traditional home baking.

Start: Lay-by at the side of the B6353 leading out of Ford towards Lowick. GR950377

This walk takes you along farm footpaths and country lanes to a plateau from which one has excellent views. The walk then visits Roughting Linn Stone, an ancient monument richly decorated with prehistoric carvings. We return across farmland and country lanes to Ford. This is one of the prettiest villages in Northumberland. Red-tiled cottages and well-kept gardens delight the eye. Overlooking the village stands Ford Castle, built in 1227 by Ordinal de Forde. A romantic tale concerns King James IV of Scotland and his connections with the castle. It is said that through dalliance here with the Lady Heron on the night before the Battle of Flodden, he lost both the battle and his life. Today the castle is a residential educational resource centre.

✤ Cross the stile to the right of a gate in the stone wall at the lay-by. A signpost next to the stile has directions for Ford Hill. Walk into the woods, and a dozen paces later turn left at a fork. The path travels through trees, below to your left is the B6353. After 100 metres the path bends to the right. Cross a bisecting track to climb some stone steps and emerge from the trees. Keep to the path with trees to your left and open fields to your right. On reaching a gate, pass through and walk down a field margin to the next gate. This allows you to emerge on a farm road. Turn left along this road, proceed for 50 metres and follow as the road bends right and through farm buildings. At the end of the buildings, turn left down a track which curves right and passes a stone-built building. This is the remains of an old mill house.

✤ Where the track divides, take the track to the right. Keep to the track as it passes to the left of a plantation. At a surfaced road, just before a bungalow, turn right and follow the road. Pass by a plantation to your left and proceed until you come to a track and a signpost to your left. The signpost bears directions for Roughting Linn and Southmoor. Turn on to this track and go through the gate. A path gently climbs along the side of a plantation to your left. At a fork take the path to the right. This descends slightly before bending to the right. To your left is Ford Moss Nature Reserve.

The reserve is the property of Northumberland Wildlife Trust and is on the site of a former mining community. In the 1860s there was a thriving community centred on the colliery, with over seventy workers employed. However, the mine began to deteriorate and by 1891 only twelve workers remained. In 1910 the mine closed. Of the community that lived here, little trace remains. The tall chimney is a silent reminder of those days.

⚘ At the next fork take the stronger path to the right and climb a slight rise. Leave this path at the point where it curves to the right. There will be a narrow path leading off left. This takes you up the slope of the hill. After a dozen paces, pass through a gate in a wire fence. The path bends right and continues its ascent of the hill. As you climb you will see the remains of an old stone quarry to your left. The path passes close to a stone wall and runs parallel with it on the last stage of the ascent. Once at the top the path leads you

Crossing Broom Ridge towards Goatscrag Hill

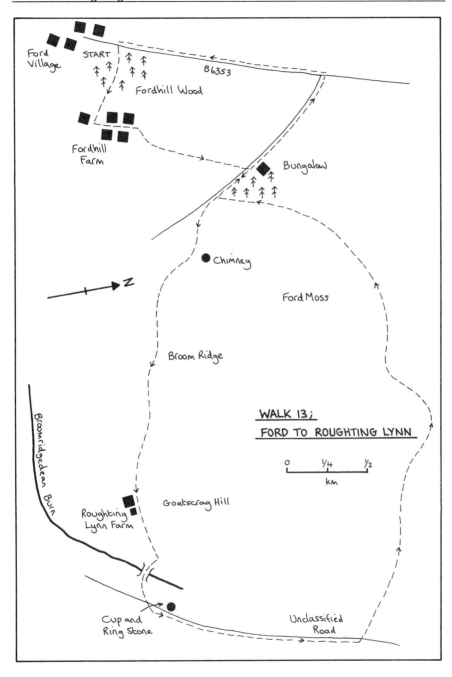

WALK 13;
FORD TO ROUGHTING LYNN

0   ¼   ½
        km

around the edge of a plateau, through bracken that can be dense in mid-summer, to a stone wall.

There are some really excellent views whilst walking across the flat summit.

↳ Turn right to descend from Goatscrag Hill. At the bottom of the descent turn left along a broad track. Pass to the left of Roughting Linn Farm. Remain on the track as it heads towards a plantation. As you near the trees, the track bends right and descends to a bridge spanning the Roughting Linn. Once across the bridge follow the track to emerge from the trees on a surfaced road.

To the left of the track after the bridge are the remains of an old settlement and fort. Both of these can be hidden under bracken and willow herb in summer.

↳ Turn left and walk along the road for 150 metres. Watch for a gap in the trees to your left. On finding it turn down the track for 200 metres to the site of the Roughting Linn Stone.

A notice next to the stone reads, 'The carved markings on this stone are one of the best examples in Northumberland of the widespread, though still unexplained, prehistoric practice of decorating large outcropping of stone with hollow cups surrounded by rings and occasionally spirals. This form of decoration, perhaps with a religious inspiration, was common from at least 3000BC or earlier. The markings are very fragile and susceptible to wear. Visitors are requested not to walk or climb upon or otherwise damage the surface of the stone. The stone is scheduled as an ancient monument.'

↳ Return to the road and turn left. Continue along the road with a plantation to your left. When the plantation ends you have clear views to either side. On coming to a signpost to the left of the road, for Southmoor and Dunsall, pass through the gate. Cross pastureland with a shallow gully to your left. At the end of the gully, walk straight ahead to a gate at the top left corner of the field. Go through the gate and turn left through another gate. Walk along the field margin with a wire fence to your right. Ahead you can see the tall chimney at Ford Moss. Remain on the field edge as the fence bends left. Pass by and ignore a small gate in the fence.

During the 19th century, farmers employed workers on a yearly contract and provided them with free accommodation. If, after the year, they did not wish to remain or not been asked to stay by the farmer, they went to the 'hirings' held in Wooler and Berwick to seek a new master. They then moved to their new job on May 12, known as 'flitting day'. Even to-day the word 'flit' exists in the Northumbrian dialect, meaning 'to move'.

↳ Where the fence makes a sharp bend to the right, walk alongside it until you come to a wicket gate on your right. Go through the gate and cross a small bridge before turning left through another wicket gate. Follow the path as it bends right through a small stand of trees, before continuing next to a wire fence on your right. Pass another small stand of trees and emerge on rough moor grass, where the path becomes stronger on the ground. At a metal gate across the path, pass through and follow a broad track to the next gate. Go through the gate and down the side of the plantation, keeping it on your right. From this point you retrace earlier steps to return to your starting point.

Local Attractions

Lady Waterford Hall in Ford village is located in the old school building. The interior walls of the school are adorned with remarkable murals painted over 100 years ago by Louisa, Marchioness of Waterford, both a talented artist and public benefactor. After the school was built she spent the following 21 years decorating it with colourful pictures depicting bible stories. Many of the figures portrayed in these scenes were adults and children resident in the village at the time. An admission fee is charged. Enquiries and opening times – 01890 820524.

Heatherslaw Light Railway is a 15' gauge steam railway running between Heatherslaw and Etal. Special Santa trains run in the Christmas period. Enquiries and opening times, telephone 01890 820244.

Heatherslaw Mill is a restored and working 19th-century corn mill. There is a gift shop and a café selling locally-produced bread, cakes and biscuits. Enquiries and opening times – 01890 820338.

14. ɦepBuRn ᴡoooꙅ círcular

Distance: 2¼ miles, 3.6km

Grade: Medium as it includes one steep climb and a descent of crags.

Maps: Ordnance Survey Landranger 75, Pathfinder 476 NU02/12

Refreshments: Chatton (3½ miles) – Percy Arms Hotel, Eglingham (6 miles) – Tankerville Arms, Wooler (8 miles) – cafés, pubs and hotels.

Start: Car park at Hepburn Woods. GR072248

The three walks that follow all begin from the car park provided by Rothbury Forests at Hepburn Woods. These woods are managed by Rothbury Forests who also manage woods at Kidland, Hepburn, Uswayford and Simonside. Walkers are welcome in all these working forests, although some areas may close temporarily to enable felling operations. Each of these three walks is different in character and introduces various aspects of interest within and around the forest area. The walk ascending Ross Castle introduces archaeology with the hill fort, local history with its anecdotes about Sir Edward Grey, and fabulous views of the Cheviot range. The other two walks are centred on the woods themselves, with excellent views and natural history. The Ros Woods walk gives beautiful seascape views whilst Hepburn Woods have a replica burial cist to view and crags to scramble over. With well-managed woodland, heather-covered grouse moor and wide open spaces, what more could one ask for from this Northumbrian landscape?

๖ From the car park, take the broad track leading off to the right of the large information board. Pass a signpost for Ros Castle and go on to a metal pole barrier across the track. Go through the gate to the right of the barrier. Follow a broad track with trees to your left and open land to your right. Soon the track curves left between rows of trees to a fork. Take the track to the left.

To the right of the fork is an interesting replica of a 3500-year-old cist. These were ancient burial chambers with four sides made of stone slabs and capped by a large slab of stone. The dead would be buried in the foetal position with various items to use in the afterlife.

๖ Walk on through the trees to pass by a marker post bearing red, green and yellow arrows. At the next fork you again take the left fork. There will be a

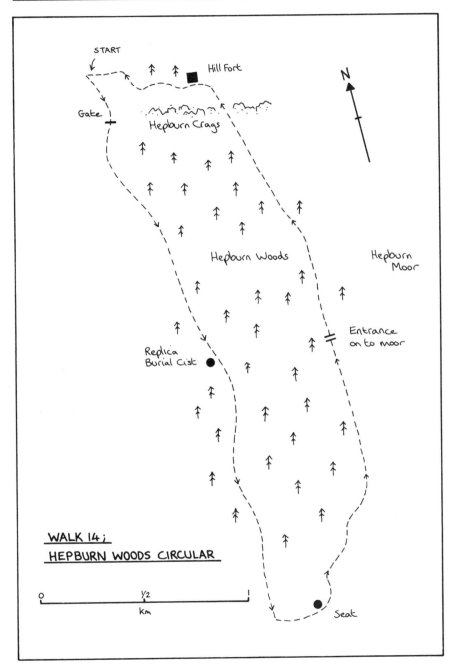

START

Hill Fort

N

Gate

Hepburn Crags

Hepburn Woods

Hepburn Moor

Entrance
on to moor

Replica
Burial Cist

WALK 14;
HEPBURN WOODS CIRCULAR

0   ½ |
km

Seat

marker post at this point with a red arrow. At the next marker post turn left, as indicated by a red arrow, thus leaving the track. A grassy path ascends steeply through trees. At the next marker post bear half left as indicated and continue climbing as the narrow path winds through dense forestry. On nearing the top of the climb the path travels through bracken. You will eventually reach the top, I promise you, although at times it seems as if the climb will never end. Now that you are at the top there only remains to pass through a gate in a wire fence. Well done!

Pause and catch your breath here, as you are rewarded with a fabulous view.

↳ After passing through the gate, you follow a well-defined track through bracken and on to heather moor. Keep parallel to Hepburn Woods on your left. The path passes a wooden picnic table before arriving at the head of Hepburn Crags.

There was a small hill fort sited here around 2000BC. It is another fine vantage point.

↳ A rocky path winds down the face of the crags. **Take care as the going is rough in places** and can be slippery after wet weather. At the base of the crags the path leads to a gate leading into the woods. Go through the gate and down a steep dirt path. There is a handrail provided to assist you. The path emerges on a broad forestry road. Turn right and follow the track to return to your starting point.

Local Attractions

Chillingham Wild Cattle have been at Chillingham Park for over 700 years. These cattle are thought to be the descendants of wild auroche that lived in the area during prehistoric times. Enquiries and opening times, telephone 01668 215250.

1ſ. bepBuRn wooᴅs to Ross castle bill foRt

Distance: 1¾ miles, 3km
Grade: Easy
Maps: Ordnance Survey Landranger 75, Pathfinder 476 NU02/12
Refreshments: Chatton (3½ miles) – Percy Arms Hotel, Eglingham (6 miles) – Tankerville Arms, Wooler (8 miles) – pubs, hotels and cafés.
Start: Hepburn Woods car park. GR072248

This walk takes you on a short climb up crags and across heather moorland to visit a prehistoric hill fort commanding excellent views of the surrounding countryside.

↳ Proceed to the right of the large Rothbury Forests information board on a rough forest track. On reaching a signpost bearing directions for Ross Castle, turn left and leave the forest road. A path takes you through gorse bushes and across a short stretch of grass before entering trees. The path climbs to a fence that you cross via a stile. There is a large boulder to the left of the stile and a signpost for Ross Castle. A narrow, twisting path travels through bracken before splitting in two. Take the path to the right and pass a second marker post for Ross Castle. Keep to the path as it climbs steadily, angling to the right, until you reach the foot of Hepburn Crags. The path bends sharply right around an old elder tree then makes an ascent to the top of the crags.

At the top, pause to look back and admire a view that encompasses the Cheviot Hills and the countryside to the south of Wooler. On the horizon the outlines of the Simonside Hills are visible on a clear day. A prehistoric hill fort occupied this site 3000 years ago.

↳ After passing a picnic table, you come to a fork in the path. The correct path is the one to the left, which climbs through bracken to a wooden marker post. Turn left as indicated by an orange arrow on the marker post.

Ahead of you rises Ross Hill. To your left the trees of Chillingham Forest are seen.

↳ The path crosses heather grouse moor to a narrow surfaced road. Cross the road and proceed to the marker post in front of you. Continue on as directed over a grassy path. From the foot of Ross Hill the path climbs steeply before bending to the right and circling the hill.

The approach track to Ross Hill

As you climb the view to your right gradually opens. On clear days the North Sea can be seen twinkling on the horizon. Holy Island and the Farne Islands will also be visible.

↳ The path finally bends left before making its final ascent to the summit.

Ross Hill fort dates from prehistoric times and comprises of ditches and a rampart surrounding the summit, with an entrance to the east. From the summit it is possible on a clear day to see six castles, these being the castles at Bamburgh, Dunstanburgh, Lindisfarne, Chillingham, Alnwick and Ford. There is an Ordnance Survey column on the summit. Attached to the side is a plaque which reads, 'Ross Castle Camp. This height, with its wide prospect, was a favourite resort of Sir Edward Grey, afterwards Viscount Grey of Follodon KG, Foreign Secretary Dec 1905 to Dec 1915. In 1956 it was presented to the National Trust as part of the national memorial to him.'

↳ When you are ready to return, retrace your steps to the narrow surfaced road. Turn right and follow the road for 900 metres as it descends to return you to the car park and the start of your walk.

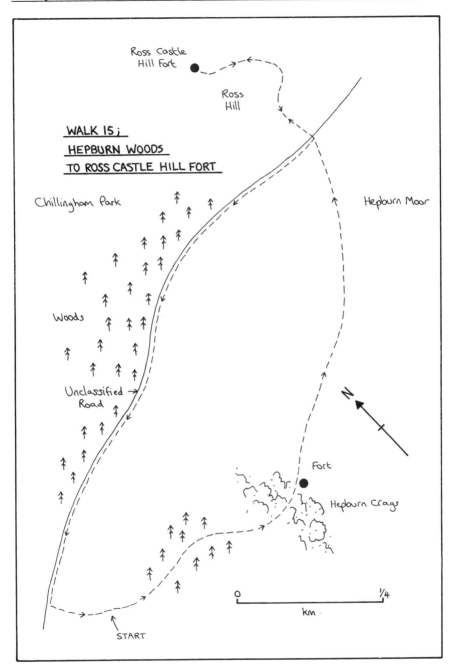

Local Attractions

Chillingham Castle is a medieval castle with Tudor additions. It has been the home of the Grey family for over 700 years. The castle stands in beautiful grounds with a lake, Italian formal garden and woodland walks. The castle is open to the public. A tour inside the castle includes the dungeons and torture room for those brave at heart. A gift shop, café and parking are available. Enquiries and opening times, telephone 01668 215359.

16. hepburn woods to ros hill woods

Distance: 5 miles, 8km

Grade: Medium

Maps: Ordnance Survey Landranger 75, Pathfinder 476 NU02/12

Refreshments: Chatton (3½ miles) – The Percy Arms Hotel, Eglingham (6 miles) – The Tankerville Arms, Wooler (8 miles) – pubs, hotels and cafés.

Start: Car park at Hepburn Woods. GR072248

This woodland walk is on well-defined paths with fine views of the Cheviot Hills and the coastal plain towards the North Sea.

✎ From the parking area, pass to the right of the large Rothbury Forests information board and follow a forestry road. Pass by a signpost for Ros Castle. On coming to a wooden marker post to the left of the road, prior to a barrier pole across the track, turn left. A narrow track ascends through trees. As the ascent is steep, a handrail has been provided to assist you. Cross a stile in a wire fence and follow a narrow path through bracken to the base of Hepburn

Hepburn Wood starting point, at the car park

Crags. The path twists and bends as it steeply ascends the crags to the summit.

A small prehistoric fort once stood here on the summit. The view to the west is tremendous as you overlook the countryside towards the Cheviot Hills.

↳ From the summit, pass by a wooden picnic table. Where the path forks, take the left fork. This rises gently through bracken before joining with a well-defined track over heather grouse moor. When you come to a surfaced road, cross and take the path to Ros Hill, seen ahead. The path climbs before contouring right and climbing steeply over peat and heather to the summit.

In prehistoric times, a fort consisting of earthworks and ramparts occupied the summit. There is an Ordnance Survey column on the summit. These triangulation columns are now obsolete as mapmakers today mainly rely upon satellite observations.

↳ Turn right from the summit and descend a path which runs parallel to a stone wall on your left. The fist stage of the descent is eased by using steps cut into the hillside. Pass a wooden marker post bearing an orange arrow whilst climbing a slight slope. At the top, go through a gate in a wire fence. Keep to the path as it descends towards Ros Hill Woods that become visible to your right.

Some really fine views of the coast are seen towards the latter part of this section. Bamburgh Castle stands out proudly on the coastline, as do the Farne Islands and Holy Island.

↳ On approaching the woods, the path leads down the left side of the trees. There will be a stone wall to your left enclosing another plantation. Remain on the path, with marker posts along the way reassuring you as you go. Pass by a gate in the stone wall, but do not go through it.

To the side of the gate you will notice a boundary stone. These large stones were used to define boundaries between different landowners. This stone has the initial N on one side and T on the other with the date 1859.

↳ Where the wall ends, a wire fence replaces it. The path climbs a slight slope to an excellent viewpoint overlooking Chillingham Forest to your left. The path then descends to a signpost bearing directions for Ros Hill Woods. Turn right to follow a broad track into the trees.

Whilst walking though Ros Hill Woods you may catch sight of some of the dragonflies that inhabit the area. Many are quite large and beauti-

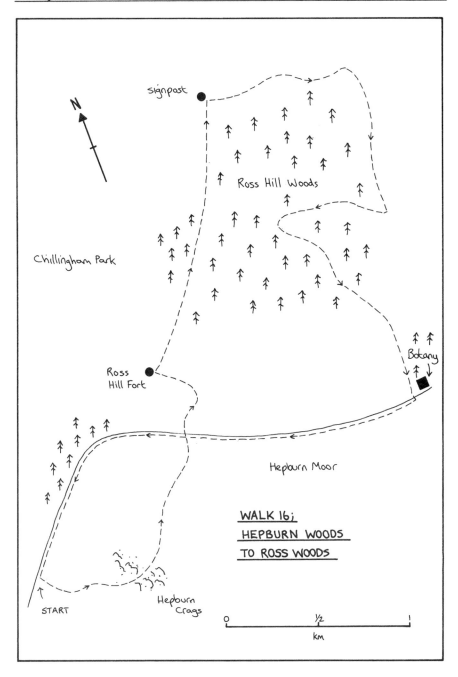

N

Signpost

Ross Hill Woods

Chillingham Park

Botany

Ross
Hill Fort

Hepburn Moor

WALK 16;
HEPBURN WOODS
TO ROSS WOODS

START

Hepburn
Crags

0   ½   1
km

fully coloured. Dragonflies can frequently be seen in heathland and the surrounding countryside. They eat smaller insects, snatching them from the air during flight.

↳ Marker posts guide you through the wood to emerge at a wire fence. Turn right and walk along the side of the fence, keeping the trees to your right.

Looking over the fence you can see the tall mast of Chatton Relay Station. This transmits BBC and ITV programmes for Glendale and the surrounding area.

↳ On coming to a marker post bearing an orange arrow, turn right as indicated. A path leads along the edge of the woods before curving left. At the next marker post turn right to re-enter Ros Hill Woods. A broad path takes you through the trees to the next marker post, where you turn left. Keep to this path to emerge from the woods at a wire fence. Cross via a stile to the left of the gate. Walk on with the fence to your left, and pass to the right of a small plantation. At a surfaced road turn right and follow this road for one and a quarter miles to return to your starting point.

Local Attractions

Chillingham Castle and Chillingham Wild Cattle. Details of both these attractions can be found at the end of the two previous walks from Hepburn Woods.

17. hethpool to dunsdale

Distance: 10½ miles, 17 km

Grade: Strenuous

Maps: Ordnance Survey Landranger 74, Pathfinder 475 NT82/92, Outdoor Leisure 16

Refreshments: Wooler (7 miles) – cafés, pubs and hotels. Milfield (8 miles) – Milfield Country Café.

Start: Visitors' car park at Hethpool. GR894281

A superb route begins with a scenic walk up the beautiful College Valley. The valley, surrounded by high, rolling green hills, is one of the most beautiful of the Cheviot valleys. This is followed by a walk through woodland to the flank of the Cheviot, passing Dunsdale at its foot. Return along the Lambden Valley with its impressive towering crags, and then back into the College Valley to return to the car pack at Hethpool.

↳ From the parking area, turn left to follow a private road up the College Valley. Remain on this road through high hills, enjoying the upland scenery for about 3 miles until you reach the College Valley Hall. Here the road forks. Take the road to the right and pass the circular stone enclosure of the RAF memorial.

The RAF memorial was built 1994-1995, and unveiled by the Duke of Gloucester on May 19, 1995. It is dedicated to the wartime aircrews who lost their lives in the Cheviot Hills. A polished stone plinth inside the enclosure lists the names of the 35 airmen who died in these hills between 1939 and 1945. Graves of German aircrew can be found in the churchyard of St Gregory's Church at nearby Kirknewton.

↳ The road climbs to contour the side of Blackhagg Rig before dropping to pass through the farm buildings of Fleehope. After Fleehope, keep to the road for just over half a mile to reach the last gate before Mounthooly. Pass through the gate. At a fork just before the white bungalow of Mounthooly, take the track to the right which passes to the rear of the bungalow.

There is a bunkhouse in a converted farmhouse beside the bungalow. It can accommodate walkers exploring the area. The bunkhouse caters for single walkers and groups of up to 25. Phone 01668 216358 for further details or to book accommodation.

↳ Once past Mounthooly, the track continues along the bottom edge of a conifer plantation and through gates to emerge on upland pasture. At a wire fence across the track, go through the gate provided.

The area to the right after the gate is the site of newly planted (1995) broad-leaved trees. Thirty-five hectares of forestry were felled to enable the planting of 70 hectares of native broad-leaved trees. This project is aimed to recreate the natural vegetation of the area. The scheme was grant-aided by Northumberland National Park and the Forestry Authority.

↳ After passing through the gate, walk on 25 metres to a marker post. Turn left down an incline to ford the College Burn. Climb the bank on the other side. Pass to the left of a sheepfold, and after 50 metres turn left at a wooden post. Descend a dip to ford the narrow Braydon Burn, which has its source high up on Braydon Crags. Continue along the flank of Cheviot on a path which rises gradually towards the top corner of the conifer plantation ahead. A few metres before you get to the corner of the trees, climb a ladder stile over a high deer fence. This stile is of necessity rather high to clear the fence.

The fence was erected to prevent deer and sheep from consuming the newly planted trees within the enclosed area. They find the young, tender trees provide a tasty morsel. Without the protection of a fence the trees would stand no chance of growth. As it is a cold climate growth is slow and patchy.

↳ Ignore a gate to your right and cross a stile leading into the trees. A narrow path threads through the trees for 300 metres before bending right to a wire fence. Walk parallel to the fence with the plantation to your left and open ground to your right. Pass an old metal shed. On reaching a stile in the fence bearing a yellow arrow, cross over. Bear half left across rough moorland, aiming for the right-hand side of the coniferous plantation ahead.

On the flank of Cheviot to your right are found several rare plants which are locally common. These include the common butterwort and the beautiful bog aspidel. The butterwort flourishes in bogs, wet heaths and among wet rocks. Its pale green leaves are covered in sticky hairs for trapping and digesting small vertebrates such as midges and flies. It then absorbs the nitrogen from them to enable growth. The yellow-leafed bog aspidel also prefers wet ground, often becoming dominant on blanket bogs. Both these plants are unusual in that they prefer soils which are deficient in nitrogen. Higher up, on more exposed ground, alpine flora flourishes, such as mountain saxifrage and thyme.

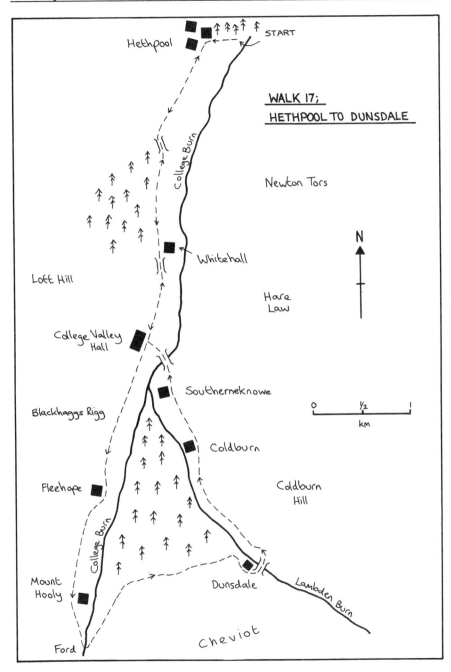

START

Hethpool

WALK 17;
HETHPOOL TO DUNSDALE

College Burn

Newton Tors

Whitehall

Loft Hill

N

College Valley
Hall

Hare
Law

Southerneknowe

Blackhaggs Rigg

0   ½   1
km

Coldburn

Coldburn
Hill

Fleehope

College Burn

Mount
Hooly

Dunsdale

Lambden Burn

Ford

Cheviot

↳ On reaching a fence cross the stile, turn right and then left to walk down the side of the trees. There will be a wire fence and open ground to your right. As you progress the path descends into the Lambden Valley and curves to the right. On reaching a stile in the fence cross over and turn left to continue descending.

From here, looking right, the Lambden Valley stretches up as far as Goldscleugh. At a gap in the trees where the electricity wires pass through you can see down the valley to Coldburn and Southernknowe. Behind them rises Blackhaggs Rig, and to its right is the tree-clad slope of Loft Hill.

↳ At the foot of the descent you will see a marker post where you turn right and go through a gate. Follow a track down towards the white-painted shepherd's house at Dunsdale.

Looking up to your right there is an excellent view of The Bizzle. The Bizzle is a massive chasm in the side of Cheviot. It was formed by the scouring action of local glaciers towards the end of the last Ice Age, after the main sheet of ice had melted.

↳ Pass to the right of the houses and through gates to a narrow surfaced

Looking along the Lambden Valley towards Dunsdale

road. Cross a bridge spanning the Bizzle Burn before the road curves left down to a bridge spanning the Lambden Burn. Cross this ridge and turn left to follow the surfaced road down the valley. You will pass under Dunsdale Crags and the impressive gliders on the slope of Coldburn Hill.

Gliders, or scree, is a slope of loose stones. The stones were created by the constant freezing and thawing of rocks thousands of years ago, during the last Ice Age.

✎ After passing Coldburn and Southernknowe the road dips and bends to cross a wooden bridge spanning the College Burn. Continue along the road to College Valley Hall.

College Valley Hall is used for regular dances and community activities. It is locally known as the 'Cuddy Stane Hall' because of its near proximity to the 'cuddy stane', a prominent boundary stone outside the hall.

✎ Turn right at the hall and enjoy a leisurely stroll down the narrow road, absorbing the scenery as you return to your starting point.

18. hethpool to newton tors

Distance: 9½ miles, 15.2km

Grade: Strenuous

Maps: Ordnance Survey Landranger 74, Pathfinder 475 NT82/92, Outdoor Leisure 16

Refreshments: Wooler (7 miles) – pubs, hotels and cafés. Milfield (8miles) – Milfield Country Café.

Start: Visitors' car park just past the cottages of Hethpool. GR894281

This dramatic walk starts from Hethpool with its quaint cottages. Their colourful gardens are soon left behind as you climb the heights of Newton Tors. As you ascend you are rewarded with impressive views across the Milfield Plain to the coast and far into the Scottish lowlands. Take your time as you descend back into the College Valley and meander along this glacial valley to return to your starting point.

✳ Turn right from the parking area to cross a cattle grid. Keep a stone wall to your right as you walk down the road to the cottages at Hethpool. When you reach a gate in the wall signposted for Old Yeavering, go through and follow the broad track along a field edge.

Built in 1910, the picturesque cottages with their well-kept gardens replace the original cottages at Hethpool. Records of Hethpool exist dating back to 1242, when the hamlet was known as Hetpol. In the Lay Subsidy Roll of 1296 some eighteen persons were recorded as living there.

✳ Continue along the track, which develops into a descending concrete ramp. Thirty metres after the ramp ends, cross a stile in the fence to your left to enter a large paddock.

Ahead and slightly to the left is the oak-clad hill of Hethpool Bell. The oak trees are said to have been planted by the famous Admiral Lord Collingwood. The oaks were intended to be used as 'navy timber', for building ships for the Royal Navy. Unfortunately, the trees did not thrive and consequently were never used.

✳ Head for a gate in a stone wall at the other side of the paddock. Pass through the gate and across rough pasture. Follow a narrow path to a plank bridge across a small stream. Cross the stream and turn slightly right to climb

The Tors from Hethpool

the bank. The path leads to a wire fence, which is crossed using the stile provided. A few metres on a wooden footbridge assists you across another stream.

Roe deer inhabit Hethpool Bell to your left. The deer may often be seen in the early morning or late evening, when they descend to lower ground foraging for food and water. Green woodpeckers are resident amongst the old oaks. Their cry, like laughter, is frequently heard as they hunt for insects in the old timber.

↳ After crossing the footbridge, turn right and then walk parallel to a stone wall on your right. The wall is soon replaced by a wire fence. At the end of the fence a rushing roar from the College Burn on your right will attract you to the waterfalls of Hethpool Linn.

A narrow track will be seen leading through gorse to your right. This takes you to a rock ledge where the tumbling cascades are seen to best advantage. Take care not to approach too near the edge and suddenly end your walk. Return to the main path.

↳ At a fork take the path to the right and go down a short slope to a gated wooden footbridge spanning the College Burn. Cross the bridge, closing the gate behind you. A path climbs left through trees to a wire fence. Cross the stile and turn right, climbing steeply out of the College Valley. At the top, pass through a gap in an old stone wall and follow a path with a wire fence to your right. To your left there is a deep, tree-clad gorge.

Looking ahead you have a clear view of the twin peaks of Newton Tors. The summit to the left is that of Easter Tor at 1420ft, and the one to the right is that of Wester Tor, the higher at 1760ft.

↳ On reaching a wooden marker post, bear half left as indicated by the yellow direction arrow. The path descends into a small gully and fords a small stream before climbing out.

Take care as the path out of the gully is lined with gorse – the thorns of which are very sharp.

↳ The path leads to a wire fence crossed by a stile. Bear half left to pass to the right of a stone sheepfold. At the marker post continue as directed to a broad track which is a permissive way. Turn left, following the track as it climbs a slope to a conifer plantation. Remain on the track through the trees and exit the plantation to pass to the right of the house and farm buildings of Kirknewton Tors.

Kirknewton Tors is marked on some maps as Torlehouses.

↳ Follow the track to a marker post on your right a few metres before a cattle grid. Turn right onto a track parallel to a stone wall on your left and head towards a gate. Pass through the gate.

To the side of this gate is a notice: 'Please take care. Some of the ground nesting birds that breed here during the spring are easily disturbed by people and more so by dogs. During April, May and June you can help minimise such disturbances by keeping dogs on a lead and keeping to the paths. Your co-operation is much appreciated. Enjoy your walk.'

↳ The path bends left then right to climb a steep, grassy slope. Remain parallel with the wall on your left to reach a stile. Cross the wall at this point via the stile. A broad path curves to the right, taking you along the top of a valley which drops away to your left.

Across the valley is Yeavering Bell. On the summit are the remains of a large, prehistoric hill fort. The stone ramparts which surround it are still visible today. The walker may be fortunate at this point to see some of the wild goats which are to be found in this area. These are not really wild but feral. They are believed to be the descendants of goats once kept for milk during Roman times.

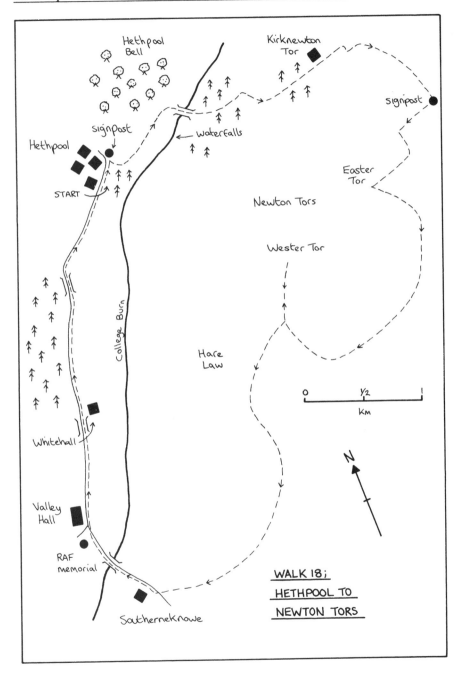

Hethpool
Bell

Kirknewton
Tor

signpost

Hethpool

signpost

Waterfalls

Easter
Tor

START

Newton Tors

College Burn

Wester Tor

Hare
Law

0   ½
km

Whitehall

N

Valley
Hall

RAF
memorial

WALK 18;
HETHPOOL TO
NEWTON TORS

Southerneknowe

✎ Stay on the track until you come to a low signpost bearing directions for Wester Tor. Turn right as directed and cross a few metres of grass to a stile set in a stone wall. Cross the stile and climb a gentle slope. Pass by a wooden marker post and keep to the path as it makes for a sheepfold ahead.

This stretch of walking provides many fine views to your right encompassing both Northumberland and part of Scotland.

✎ Where the path descends a slight dip and the sheepfold disappears from sight, the path turns left to rise towards the shoulder of the hill. Near the top, pass a marker post and walk on to the next one. At this post is a low signpost. Turn right, as indicated for Easter Tors, and cross heather moor to the summit of Easter Tor. On the summit you will find a signpost for Wester Tor.

Turn right at the signpost to arrive at an impressive viewing point. The view overlooks the Milfield Plain and the Northumbrian coastline. Looking towards Scotland you can see the Eildon Hills near Melrose, and further north the Lammermuir Hills. Below to your right there are good views of the ramparts encircling Yeavering Bell. In my opinion this has to be one of the best viewpoints in the Cheviots.

✎ Walk back to the last signpost and head in the direction indicated for Wester Tor. Wooden marker posts with yellow arrows guide you across heather moor. At a low signpost to the left of the path, turn right, as indicated for Wester Tor. The path is well defined and curves around the side of Wester Tor. On passing a further signpost the path forks. Take the fork to the right to continue curving around the hill before ascending towards the summit of Wester Tor. At the next low signpost turn right as directed and go on to the summit.

Here again spectacular views greet the walker. Mere words cannot fully describe the sheer grandeur. You really have to go there to experience it yourself.

✎ From the summit walk back to the last signpost. Go through a gate in the wire fence and descend Hare Law, keeping an old stone wall to your left. A wire fence replaces the wall as you approach a signpost next to a stile in the fence. The signpost bears directions for Southernknowe. Take the direction indicated for Southernknowe. Keep a wire fence to your left for 200 metres before crossing a stile on to heather moor. The wire fence, now on your right, is followed to the field corner. Leave the fence and bear half left across moorland. After 100 metres pass a wooden marker post bearing a yellow arrow. The path bends right and then left as it descends to a narrow, surfaced road.

The descent is rather steep in places and care should be exercised when ground conditions are wet or poor. The valley to your left is the Lambden Valley.

↳ At the surfaced road turn right and go through a gate. Pass the buildings of Southernknowe. The road dips to cross a bridge spanning the College Burn then rises to the College Valley Hall.

To the left of the College Valley Hall is a large, circular, stone enclosure. This is the RAF Memorial to the wartime aircrews who lost their lives in the Cheviot Hills. A polished stone plinth within the enclosure lists the names of the thirty-five aircrew who died in these hills between 1939 and 1945.

↳ Turn right at the hall and follow a narrow, surfaced road which runs down the valley and returns you to the starting point.

19. holy island circular

Distance: 4½ miles, 7.2km

Grade: Easy

Maps: Ordnance Survey Landranger 75, Pathfinder 452 NU04/14

Refreshments: These are readily available in the village with a variety of cafés, pubs and hotels. Try home-made crab and salmon sandwiches. The seafood caught locally in season is delicious.

Start: Holy Island car park. GR127422

Holy Island, or Lindisfarne, is regarded as the seat of early Christianity in the northern kingdoms, and since the 7th century has been a cradle of religious culture and inspiration. Today it is still a place of pilgrimage for all denominations. It is a true island, being cut off from the mainland twice a day. The causeway that links it with the mainland is submerged at high tide by deep water. It is imperative to check the tide tables before embarking on a journey to Holy Island. Safe crossing times are on display at local tourist offices and on a

Lindisfarne Castle

board prior to the causeway. Do not take chances. Many foolish motorists have been forced to abandon their vehicles and seek safety in the refuge hut provided, only to watch their vehicle sink below the sea. The walk explores the village and the ruined priory, famous for its connections with St Cuthbert and St Aidan and the Lindisfarne Gospels, before visiting Lindisfarne Castle and returning along a shoreline walk.

✎ Turn right on leaving the car park and proceed to the road junction. Turn left to pass a café, and at the T-junction turn right. Pass the Castle Inn and the local post office before turning left at the top of the road. Walk on past Lindisfarne Craft Shop and Winery on your left.

Lindisfarne mead, made on the island, is exported throughout the world. Made with honey and herbs, the mead was traditionally given to newly-weds as an aphrodisiac. Free tasting is available on the premises, as well as a selection of products containing mead, such as fudge and marmalade.

✎ Continue along the road until you reach the cemetery wall surrounding the church of St Mary. Pass through a gate set in the wall and enter the churchyard.

As a slight diversion you can continue down this lane till you come to the rocky beach where you can see the tiny island of St Cuthbert. It can be approached at low tide. St Cuthbert spent time on the island in solitude to commune with nature and God. Later, even this isolation was not sufficient and he moved to a hermitage on the nearby Farne Islands. Tradition has it that St Cuthbert was very fond of eider ducks, which are common on these shores. So much so that they have become known locally as Cuddy's ducks.

✎ A narrow, surfaced path takes you through the graveyard and around the side of the church. It passes the ruins of Lindisfarne Priory before emerging in the village square.

The church of St Mary dates from the 13th century and contains replicas of the Book of Kells and the Lindisfarne Gospels. An illustrated display demonstrates the history of these priceless books. Lindisfarne Priory dates from the 11th century and is built mainly from red sandstone. St Aidan and his monks built a priory here in AD634. Sadly, some 200 years later the Vikings destroyed the priory. In 1537 Henry VII dissolved the Priory during his dissolution of the monasteries and the building became a military garrison. The soldiers stationed there looted and destroyed the building. Today it is cared for by English Heritage.

↳ After emerging from the graveyard, turn right past the village square towards the white- painted Crown and Anchor Hotel. Go down a narrow gap to the right of the hotel towards a turnstile gate. Pass through the gate and along a surfaced path across a meadow to another turnstile gate. Once through this gate, turn left towards the old harbour and follow a broad track along the shore to a surfaced road.

Around the harbour can be seen large, upturned wooden boats. In earlier times these boats formed houses for local fishermen and their families. They are now registered as listed buildings and used to store fishing equipment. Lobster and crab pots are evidence of the shellfishing industry, although salmon fishing is the mainstay of the fishing community.

↳ Turn right and follow the road as it leads you towards Lindisfarne Castle. Just before the castle you go through a kissing gate to a cobbled path. After taking a few paces, the path forks. Take the path to the right, which gently climbs and contours around the base of the castle walls. To your right are fine seascape views towards the mainland.

Lindisfarne Castle is not an ancient edifice. The castle was built on these crags in 1550, as an artillery fort to protect the harbour. Stones from the priory were utilised in its construction. In 1902 it was extensively modified by Sir Edward Lutyens to create a private residence for Edward Hudson, founder of Country Living magazine. In 1944 Sir Edward de Stein and his sister gave the castle to the National Trust.

↳ Where the path bends left to the entrance of the castle, keep straight ahead to leave the path and cross short-cropped grass to a stone enclosure, ahead and slightly to the right.

The stone enclosure surrounds old limekilns. Steps take you down to the base of the kilns where an excellent interpretative panel explains how they built and operated them. The kilns were built in 1860. Limestone from a quarry in the north of the island was delivered to the kilns via a waggon way. The limestone was then burnt with the aid of coal brought in by boat. The workings finally closed at the beginning of the 20th century.

↳ When you have explored the kilns, turn left and away from the enclosure. Cross cropped grass to a small, wooden bridge that takes you on to a raised walkway. Walk along the walkway as it curves left to a gate. Go through the

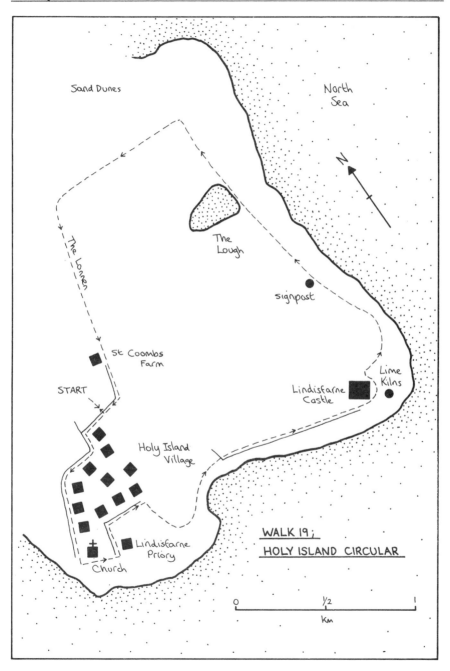

Sand Dunes

North
Sea

N

The Lough

The Lonnen

Signpost

St Coombs
Farm

START

Lindisfarne
Castle

Lime
Kilns

Holy Island
Village

Lindisfarne
Priory

Church

WALK 19;
HOLY ISLAND CIRCULAR

0   ½   1
           Km

gate and contour the cliff top. Pass by and ignore a signpost to your left and keep on to a reed-bordered lake. This lake is known as The Lough.

The lake is a nature reserve and home to numerous waterfowl. Overlooking it is a large hide that you are free to enter. The hide opened on November 25th, 1990, and is dedicated to the memory of Dr Paul Greenwood (1952 – 1988).

↳ Once past the lake, cross a stile in a fence and continue on the path to the next stile. After crossing it, turn left and follow a broad, grassy path. There will be a stone wall to your left and sand dunes to your right. Remain on the path until you come to a signpost pointing to the left. Turn left as indicated down a broad track that takes you towards Holy Island village. This is an ancient track known as The Lonnen. The track passes through the buildings of St Combe's Farm, where it becomes a surfaced road. This returns you to the start of your walk.

Local Attractions

Lindisfarne Castle was built in the 14th century as an artillery fort and was used as a garrison until 1820. The castle is open to the public and an admission fee is charged. Enquiries and opening times, telephone 01289 389244.

Lindisfarne Priory is a ruined 11th-century priory built by Benedictine monks from Durham and dedicated to St Cuthbert. An adjoining visitor centre houses an exhibition about the monks and their way of life. There is also a gift shop. An admission fee is charged. Enquiries and opening times – 01289 389200.

Museum of Island Heritage depicts the heritage of the island and contains many displays of life as it used to be. Free admission. For information on tide crossing times, telephone 01289 330733.

20. holystone to oove cRag

Distance: 4½ miles, 7.2km

Grade: Medium

Maps: Ordnance Survey Landranger 81, Pathfinder 499 NT80/90, Outdoor Leisure 16

Refreshments: The Salmon Inn in Holystone

Start: Holystone picnic area. GR951025

This delightful walk uses well-defined paths and tracks through woodland to the magical setting of Dove Crag and its waterfall. The place is traditionally reputed to be the haunt of Northumbrian fairies. Good waterproof footwear is recommended for this walk as paths can be muddy after rain.

᭾ From the car park, go up the narrow, surfaced road and through a gate across the road. Remain on this road as it skirts along the side of a plantation to your right. To your left you have fine views over a broad, shallow valley.

This area is part of Holystone Nature Reserve. Management of the reserve is grant-aided by English Nature. The road you are walking on is built on the course of an old Roman road.

᭾ When the trees to your right end you will pass a large Forest Enterprise board to the left of the road. This reads, 'Holystone Common. Jointly managed by Forest Enterprise and Northumberland Wildlife Trust.' The road gradually climbs a slope. To your right a heather-clad slope rises to a plantation at the top. To your left the ground drops away to a plantation of Scots pine, larch and native pine.

When you reach the top of the rise, pause to look back and admire the view.

᭾ The road heads towards a plantation. When you reach a passing place for cars, the last before the plantation, look to your right for a wooden marker post. It is only a few metres from the road. On locating it, leave the road and follow a path from the post which takes you along the side of a plantation to a gap in a stone wall.

On this stretch, if you miss the post you will encounter a host of army notice boards next to a gate. This is the **entrance to a military firing**

zone and the public must not pass beyond this point when red flags are flying or red lamps displayed. Who said walking was a safe hobby!

✍ Pass through the gap on to a well-defined path which takes you through the trees to a red-stoned forest road. A few paces on, leave the road on a path to your left through the trees. Remain on the path as it curves right. Pass a marker post to your right. At the next post bear half left uphill, and pass a heather-clad slope to your left.

After a spell of wet weather this path can be very muddy. Weatherproof footwear is recommended.

✍ At a marker post bearing a yellow arrow, continue straight ahead and past it to cross a shallow ditch to enter trees. A few dozen paces takes you to a marker post. Pass by and notice the open area to your left where the rocks of Dove Crag rise before you. At the next post turn left and up a slope on a narrow, winding path through heather and large rocks. This takes you to the foot of a waterfall.

This area around Dove Crag is reputed to be the home of fairies, and the overall atmosphere of the place makes one think there may be some truth in the old folk lore. However, if you visit this place in autumn when the trees are bare, then the atmosphere is different. One gets the feeling this may be more the haunt of witches and goblins than fairies. A number of yew trees planted around the area reinforce this feeling. Yew trees were traditionally planted in graveyards to ward off evil. Perhaps these here were planted to ward off something evil around the falls.

✍ Return to the last marker post and turn left to re-enter the trees. The path curves right and leads to a marker post. Here we join a public footpath and turn left. At a fork in the path take the path to the left posted as a public footpath. Pass through conifers to emerge on a red-stone forestry road. Turn left and follow the road. At the point where the road curves sharply to the left, turn half right onto a lesser track. After a few metres the red stone peters out to become a grass track. There will be a wooden seat to your left.

This seat is sited to take advantage of the excellent view to the north through the trees.

✍ Turn right to pass a marker post, then go along a path through the trees. This is a long straight stretch of about half a mile. At its end turn sharp right. Pass a marker post before the path bends left and then right. At the foot of a descent turn left and go through a stretch of old, gnarled oak trees. In early summer the trees are alive with birdsong. The path bends right to descend

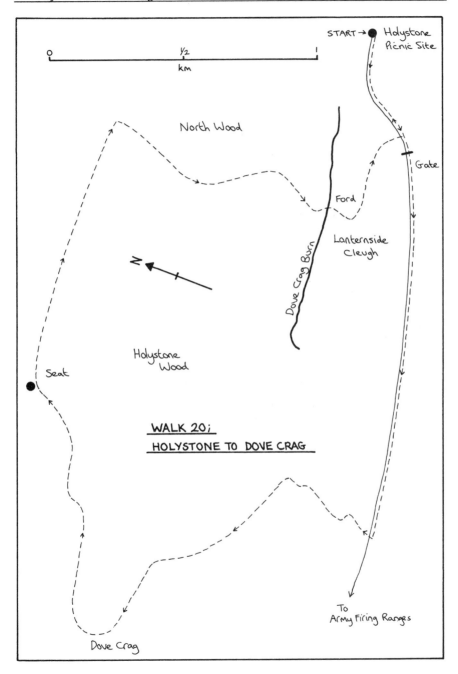

START → Holystone Picnic Site

0   ½   1
km

North Wood

Gate

Ford

Lanternside Cleugh

Dove Crag Burn

N

Holystone Wood

Seat

WALK 20;

HOLYSTONE TO DOVE CRAG

To Army Firing Ranges

Dove Crag

under a broad canopy of copper beech trees. These are at their best in the late autumn sunshine.

Beech and oak were once managed by coppicing. Shoots were allowed to grow from the stump after the tree was felled. The shoots grew to produce long poles which were then cut and burnt to produce charcoal. The regular cutting cycle favoured wildlife because of the number of mini-habitats created.

↳ At the foot of the descent there will be a field. Turn right and then left at a marker post a few paces on. A path takes you down an avenue between the trees to the side of a field. At the end make a sharp turn to the right. A dozen paces on there will be a marker post to the left. Leave the path at this point and turn left to descend into a gorge. Steps cut into the slope help you on the way down. At the bottom, ford the narrow Dove Burn.

The gorge is Lanternside Cleugh. At the bottom you will find ferns, mosses and liverworts growing in profusion.

↳ Climb out of the gorge assisted by steps cut in the slope. At the top bear left along the top of the tree-clad side of Lanternside Cleugh. Pass a marker post bearing red and orange arrows. A few paces on from here the path forks. Take either path as they join up again a little further on. The path angles away from the gorge into the trees. Keep to the path as it takes you to a gate leading on to a narrow, surfaced road. Turn left down the road to return to the starting point.

Local Attractions

Lady's Well lies in a small enclosure just outside Holystone. It is a rectangular pool measuring 11.8 metres by 7.3 metres, with a stone cross in the centre. A stone table stands at one end of the pool and a statue of Paulinus at the other. In AD627 it is reputed that Bishop Paulinus baptised 3000 Northumbrians in this pool over the Easter period. It is probable that this spring had its origins in pagan times, when water spirits were venerated. This is a beautiful spot to rest and meditate.

21. holystone woods círcular

Distance: 2 miles, 3.2km

Grade: Easy

Maps: Ordnance Survey Landranger 81, Pathfinder 499 NT80/90, Outdoor Leisure 16

Refreshments: The Salmon Inn in Holystone.

Start: Holystone Woods picnic area car park. GR 951025

A short, pleasant walk following well-defined forest tracks and paths. Included in the walk is a visit to the holy site of Lady's Well, followed by a woodland walk and then a descent into a pretty, wooded gorge. This is an ideal walk for the family, perfect for working off that Sunday dinner.

❧ From the car park, go up the track to the right of the large information board. Pass through the gate and follow a broad track through Norway spruce trees. On coming to a signpost bearing directions for Lady's Well, turn right and leave the track. A path leads through trees to emerge in a field. Cross the field and ford a narrow stream. Go to the right of a small stand of trees enclosed by a stone wall. Turn left on reaching a farm track and go through a gate. The entrance to Lady's Well is in front of you.

The well is also known as St Ninian's Well. It once belonged to a priory of nuns which existed in Holystone during the 12th century. Before this it had been a well-used watering place since Roman times for travellers using the nearby Roman road from Redesdale to the coast. It is reputed that in AD627 Paulinus baptised 3000 Northumbrians in the waters of the well over the Easter period.

❧ Retrace your steps back to the signpost for Lady's Well. Turn right and keep to the track as it gradually climbs through trees before curving to the left. Pass through an area of old, gnarled oak trees, this is part of North Wood.

North Wood is a nature reserve jointly run with Northumberland Wildlife Trust.

❧ Continue, with a wire fence and the top of an open field to your left. Pass by a wooden seat positioned to your right.

The seat makes a fine resting place from which you can admire the view towards the Simonside Hills.

❧ Ignore a broad track leading off to the right. A few paces on, turn left at a marker post and go down an avenue between trees to the side of a field. At the end make a sharp turn to the right. A dozen paces on is a marker post.

Lady's Well

Turn left to leave the path and descend into a gorge. Steps cut in the side help you on the way down. At the bottom, ford the narrow stream of Dove Burn.

The gorge is Lanternside Cleugh. Take care after rain as the way in and out of the gorge can be slippery.

↳ Climb out of the gorge assisted by steps cut in the side. At the top, a path bends left along the top of the tree-clad gorge. Pass a marker post bearing red and orange arrows. A few paces on the path forks. Take either path as they join up a little further on. The path angles to the right, leading away from the gorge and through trees. Follow the path to a gate leading to a narrow, surfaced road. Turn left and go down the road to return to your starting point.

Local Attractions

The wood at Holystone provides a number of interesting walks. Details can be obtained in a leaflet from Rothbury Forests: 1 Walby Hill, Rothbury, Northumberland NE65 7NT. They manage a number of walks in other forests within north Northumberland.

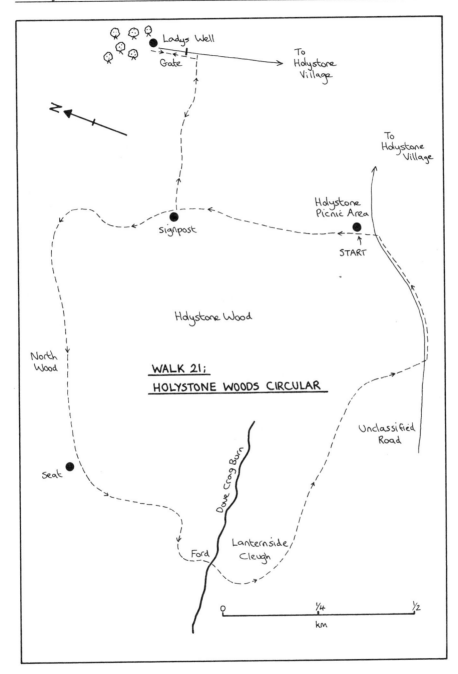

WALK 21;
HOLYSTONE WOODS CIRCULAR

22. ílɒeʀton to the ɒoɒ

Distance: 5 miles, 8km

Grade: Medium

Maps: Ordnance Survey Landrangers 75 and 81, Pathfinders 475 NT82/92 and 487 NT81/91 and 488 NU 01/11, Outdoor Leisure 16

Refreshments: Wooler (5 miles) has cafés, pubs and hotels.

Start: Ilderton village. Park carefully on grass verges. GR218219

This gem of a walk includes a new permissive footpath. This footpath provides an attractive alternative route between Harehope Burn and Ilderton to that offered by existing public footpaths. The path crosses Heddon Hill and in addition to providing excellent views of the surrounding countryside, allows walkers the chance to explore the archaeology in this area.

↳ Head west up a road passing to the left of cottages. Where the cottages end, follow the road as it bends left and proceeds along Smithy's Strip. You have a hedgerow and trees to your right. After passing through the boundary wall of Ilderton Moor Farm, walk on a dozen paces to a gate on your right.

A quaint sign on this gate reads:

If Ye Be Man, If Ye Be Woman
If Ye Be Gan Or Ye Be Comin
If Ye Be Soon Or Ye Be Late
Please Take Time To Shut The Gate.

↳ Climb over a stile to the left of this amusing gate and walk up the side of a field with a stone wall to the right. Ignore a turning right to a gate in the wall. Keep ahead to go through a clump of gorse bushes. Take care here as these bushes can be very sharp. Once through the gorse, continue up the field, next to a stone wall, until you come to a gate. Ilderton Moor Farm can be seen over the fields to your left. Cross the stile to the left of the gate and bear half left across the field to the marker post ahead.

Take care as there may be a bull in this field. Where pastureland is at a premium, farmers must use fields with public footpaths running across them. However, these *should* be beef bulls and provided you walk quietly past they are *usually* more interested in the cows then you. The wise walker will, however, keep very far away from *any* bull.

↳ At the post turn right, as directed by a white arrow on a green background, on to a permissive path which begins to ascend the slope of Heddon Hill. Where the path forks, take the path to the left leading towards the summit.

The summit trig point on Heddon Hill

As you climb the hill and near the summit, you will see to your left a large, elliptical crater. This contains the remains of a homestead dating from medieval times. Its boundary walls are well preserved and easily seen. Some 200 metres further on you will see a circular depression to the left of the path. This marks the site of an ancient settlement with hut circles. If you walk half right across the hillside from here it will bring you to the remains of another well-preserved settlement.

↳ The path curves left just below the summit, which is marked by a white trig column. The views are good to the south, extending to the distant Simonside Hills on the horizon. These dark hills, reminiscent of waves, are explored in a later walk. Descend Heddon Hill to a marker post. The Dod Farm is seen ahead in front of a small plantation.

You may be lucky enough to see a curlew flying high across this open land. The curlew, its lonesome cry echoing the solitude of the Cheviot Hills, is used as the symbol of the Northumberland National Park.

↳ Turn right at the post on to a public bridleway. Pass through a gate and go on to the next marker post. At this point turn left on to a public footpath, thus leaving the bridleway. Cross a small dip in the ground and go through the next gate to a rough farm road. Follow the road to The Dod.

Game birds and partridges are often seen in these wide open spaces. Smaller than pheasants and more timid, the partridge is becoming less common in our countryside. They are usually seen in small groups. When disturbed they fly low across the ground to cover.

♧ Turn left to pass down the side of the farm. After the last building, turn right to go through a gate and across a bridge spanning the Harelow Burn. A few paces on pass a marker post and keep straight ahead to a fork. Take the path to the left to the next marker post. Here bear half left, crossing rough grass and bracken to a wire fence. Climb the stile into an area of improved pasture before another stile returns you to moorland. A marker post directs you left to pass to the left of a large pile of stones.

These piles of stones are known as clearance cairns and are found distributed throughout the Northumbrian countryside. They date from prehistoric times to much more recent history, and are created when fields were cleared of stones by hand before they were used for agricultural purposes.

♧ A broad track takes you across heather moorland to a gate. Go through the gate and continue to pass to the right of a sheepfold adjacent to a black shed. On reaching a wide, stone farm track, turn right along it. Follow this track over a cattle grid, descending to cross a stream before climbing to another cattle grid. To your left across a field you can see the buildings of Calder Farm to the right of trees. Pass through a gate on to a narrow, surfaced road, and proceed straight ahead to a T-junction. Turn left down the road, with a stone wall to the right. On coming to a point where the road bends right, keep straight ahead on a track leading into trees. Pass a sign warning the ford is unsuitable for motor vehicles. The track narrows as it descends to a concrete footbridge spanning the Roddam Burn.

The walker may be fortunate to see some of the red squirrels which live in these woods. These elusive creatures are fast becoming rare due to the proliferation of the grey squirrel. The area around the footbridge is a sylvan spot. The nearby banks are lined with alder trees, honeysuckle, fern and other plants. Well worth a pause in the busiest of lives.

♧ Cross the bridge and climb the path to go through a gate. A grassy path bends to the right up a gentle slope and through gorse bushes to a gate. To your left is Ilderton Moor Farm. The wire enclosure is for the rearing of game birds. Pass to the right of the farm to a farm road. Remain on the road to return to your starting point.

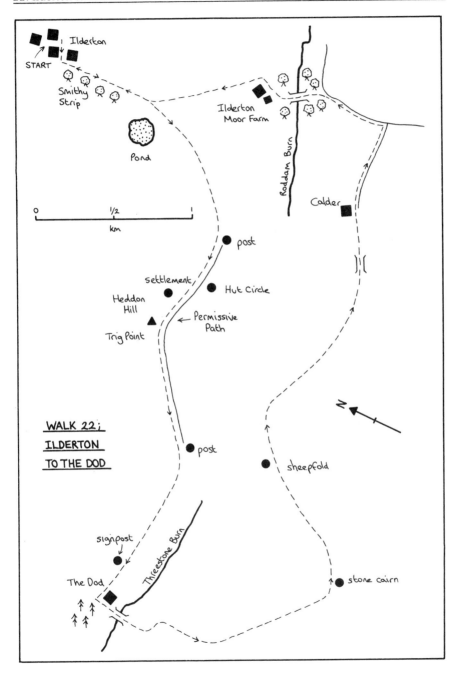

WALK 22;
ILDERTON
TO THE DOD

23. ílðerton to threestoneburn stone círcle

Distance: 11 miles, 17.5km

Grade: Strenuous

Maps: Ordnance Survey Landrangers 75 and 81, Pathfinders 475 NT82/92 and 487 NT81/91 and 488 NU01/11, Outdoor Leisure 16

Refreshments: Wooler (5 miles) has pubs, cafés and hotels.

Start: Ilderton village. Park carefully on grass verges. GR218219

This is a continuation of the walk from Ilderton to the Dod, across moor and through forest. The destination is an ancient stone circle in Threestoneburn Woods. The circle of large stones is believed to be of ceremonial significance. It dates back to 1600-1500BC.

ᗉ *Follow the directions for the walk from Ilderton to the Dod (Walk 22) until you reach The Dod, then refer to the following:*

ᗉ Just before the Dod there is a signpost to the left of the farm track. This bears directions for South Middleton, Langlee and Threestoneburn House. Turn right to follow the direction for South Middleton and head across rough moor. Aim towards a rocky outcrop with a marker post to the right of it. Pass by the post and walk on to the next. Descend a slight slope to a wire fence, which you cross using a stile. Turn left and continue descending into the pretty Lilburn Dene.

The dene is an idyllic place, with the Lilburn Burn flowing through it. Alder trees decorate the banks – the perfect place to rest and have a break by the water.

ᗉ Cross the bridge spanning the Lilburn Dene and ascend a grassy path to climb out of the dene. At the top the path goes to the left of a large, stone-built enclosure. The path drops into a hollow with a stream at the bottom. Cross a plank bridge and rise to a marker post. Once past this post, further posts guide you along.

As you walk along you will notice the humps and ridges of an old settlement in the ground to the right of the path.

ᗉ The path gradually deteriorates, but keep using the marker posts until you cross a rough stretch and arrive at the last post.

If you have any problems with the last stretch then aim for the right side

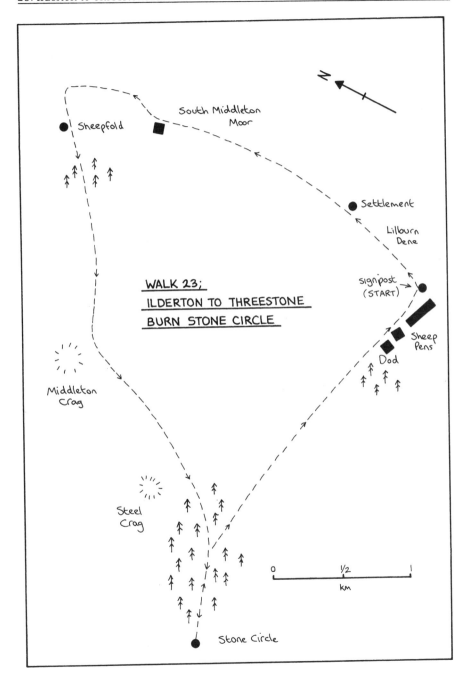

WALK 23;
ILDERTON TO THREESTONE
BURN STONE CIRCLE

The Stone Circle at Threestoneburn Woods

of a conifer plantation which can be seen ahead. Gorse bushes to the right of the trees are a reliable beacon when they are in bloom.

⮑ The path dips into Middleton Dene. Cross the stream at the bottom using the wooden footbridge and go up the other side. Pass to the right of the cottage of South Middletonmoor. At a marker post, take the right-hand path to a gate in a stone wall. Do not go through the gate. Turn left and keep next to a stone wall on your right to reach a fence across the path. Go through a gate in the fence and then on till you reach a gate in the wall. Turn left and follow a broad track. Pass to the left of a sheepfold and through a gate in a wire fence.

Looking to your left and ahead you will see the impressive jagged peaks of Middleton Crags. Sheepfolds, or stells as they are locally called, are stone-built, circular enclosures with one entrance. They are used by shepherds for the gathering and sheltering of sheep, especially so in winter when the sheep could be fed in a safe, sheltered place. They are not used much today and a large number have fallen into disrepair.

⮑ Bear half left to a plantation ahead. Cross a stile leading into the trees, a yellow arrow indicates the way. Descend into a deep hollow where you cross another stile to exit from the plantation. Climb out of the hollow to a stile in a wire fence. Cross the stile and turn half left to a marker post next to a farm track. Turn left to follow the track to a gate. Once through the gate a yellow arrow directs you ahead. The track rises gently and curves around the base of Middleton Crags to the left. At a point where the track bends right to climb the crags, continue straight ahead, leaving the track. Walk on to a gate in a fence. Pass through the gate and along a grassy path to a large plantation.

This is Threestoneburn Woods, a conifer plantation covering many acres. The conifer plantations within the Cheviots usually comprise one or more of four species of tree: the Sitka Spruce, the Norway Spruce, the Scots Pine and the Larch. All of these are ideally suited for the area with their ability to establish themselves easily and survive the often harsh winter conditions.

↳ Pass through a gate into the trees and down a heather-lined track. At a wire fence across the path, cross via a stile. A dozen paces on turn right at a marker post and follow a well-defined farm track. This track is lined with various species of trees and takes you to Threestoneburn House.

Originally a shooting lodge, the house is now used as a holiday retreat.

↳ Pass to the right of the house and across a footbridge spanning the Threestone Burn. Bear half right along a grassy path and through a gate in a wire fence. Cross another foot bridge and continue on to a stone wall. Go through the gate and turn left. Cross a small stream and walk on to the site of Threestoneburn Stone Circle.

The above footbridges are the work of Northumberland National Park Voluntary Warden Service and were erected in 1981. Of the original thirteen stones that comprised the stone circle only three of them remain in the upright position. The rest have toppled over and found rest in the grass.

↳ Retrace your steps back to Threestoneburn House and return along the track to the marker post you passed earlier. Here, instead of turning left, we continue straight on along the track. Pass through a gate and along a tree-lined track to the next gate. Once through the gate continue ahead, following the track to cross a footbridge.

This bridge is another erected in 1981 by the National Parks Voluntary Warden Service.

↳ Pass to the left of a small plantation and arrive at the entrance to the farm buildings of The Dod.

↳ *At this point refer back to the Ilderton to The Dod walk for your route to return to the starting point.*

24. kilbam farm circular

Distance: 3½ miles, 5.5km

Grade: Medium, as it involves a stiff climb to the summit of Kilham Hill

Maps: Ordnance Survey Landranger 74, Pathfinder 463 NT83/93

Refreshments: Wooler (7 miles) has numerous pubs, hotels and cafés. Milfield (6 miles) has The Country Café which provides meals and refreshments with an excellent choice.

Start: Car parking area at GR885325

This walk has been planned and made possible thanks to the generosity of the owners of the land, Kit and Christian Collins. The original medieval hamlet of Kilham was a self-contained farming settlement located in a field above the present Kilham. Only a few clumps of stone mark the site. During the troubled years of Border warfare the settlement suffered badly as it lay across the route of a reiver short cut between the Cheviots and Yetholm in Scotland. This walk takes you through Kilham and along a disused railway line before making a steep climb of Kilham Hill. Extensive views at the top make this a memorable walk.

᛭ From the area set aside as a car park, walk back down the road towards Kilham. On the way down you will notice to your right a mill pond which was restored in the 1980s. Pass by an empty stone building to your left prior to a bungalow.

This stone building was once the village bakery, providing for the needs of the farming village. Behind it there used to be a 19th-century joiner's shop which constructed wagon wheels, furniture and coffins. Kilham was once largely self-sufficient, and the cottages were very modern for their time.

᛭ As you enter Kilham, pass to the left of the farm sheds and then between the row of 19th-century cottages to arrive at a road. Cross the road and go through a gate in the stone wall. Bear half right across a field to a metal gate in the fence opposite. Go through the gate and turn right on to a former railway track. After a few paces, cross a wooden bridge over a narrow stream. The walk continues along the disused railway line. On both sides of you hawthorn, broom and ash trees delight the eye. Further down the line you pass new tree plantings on the slope to your right.

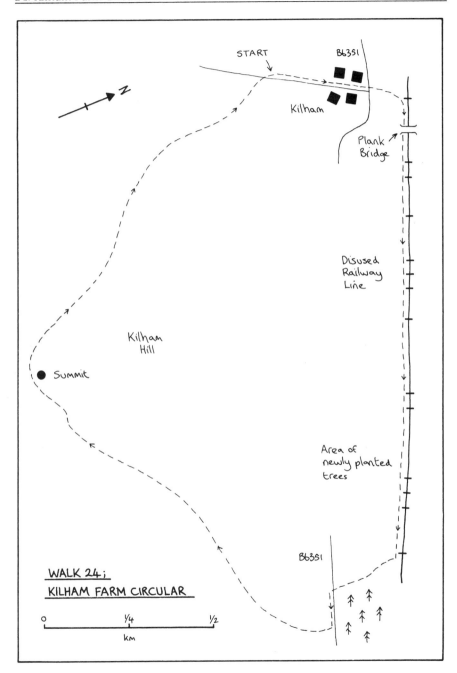

START

B6351

Kilham

Plank Bridge

Disused Railway Line

Kilham Hill

Summit

Area of newly planted trees

B6351

WALK 24;
KILHAM FARM CIRCULAR

0   ¼   ½
km

The railway line opened in 1867 and carried trains between Alnwick and Cornhill. It carried passengers till 1930, and then goods only till its closure in 1963. The overgrown hedgerows and new native tree plantings have enhanced the land, providing cover for small animals. You may be lucky and spot a kestrel or short-eared owl hunting as you pass.

↳ Continue along the line for about half a mile to reach a wire fence across the way. At this point, turn right and climb the slope through newly planted trees. At the top turn left and walk parallel to a restored stone wall on your right. On sighting a ladder stile in the wall, bear right towards it. Cross the stile to a road. Turn left and walk down the road for fifteen metres before passing through a farm gate on the opposite side of the road.

The new tree plantings are part of a woodland regeneration project by the Woodland Trust and include birch, rowan, ash, wild cherry and oak.

↳ Once through the farm gate a well-defined track takes you up the hillside to another gate set in a stone wall. After passing through the gate the track climbs a rise before making a slight dip to pass the ruins of an old farm house.

Many of these ruinous, old farm cottages were abandoned when the land was enclosed. Others became unpopular due to their isolation and lack of amenities such as electricity, a decent water supply, and telephone, etc.

↳ The route ascends with the going rather steep in places. The path bends slightly left before the cairn on the summit of Kilham Hill becomes visible. Make your way towards the prominent pile of stones marking the summit.

The view from the top of Kilham Hill is dramatic, more than compensating for the climb to get there. On a clear day it stretches deep into Scotland and across the Northumbrian coastal plain to the distant North Sea. Behind you the Cheviot range marches along the skyline.

↳ From the summit, bear half right as you descend. There is no definite path but if you make your way down towards the end of a hedge which contains oak trees and a few hawthorns and is at the base of the valley, you should find your way. Turn right on reaching the hedge and walk parallel to it. Pass through a gate and into a field. This field can be boggy after wet weather. On coming to a metal gate, pass through and turn left to ford a stream. Climb the bank on the other side and go through another metal gate to a farm road. Turn right to return to your starting point.

25. kirknewton to yeavering Bell

Distance: 6 miles, 9.6km

Grade: Strenuous

Maps: Ordnance Survey Landranger 75, Pathfinder 475 NT82/92 and 463 NT83/93, Outdoor Leisure 16

Refreshments: Wooler (6½ miles) has pubs, hotels and cafés. Milfield Country Café is at Milfield (7½ miles).

Start: Kirknewton village. Park on roadside grass verges. GR914303

This jewel of a walk culminates in a visit to Yeavering Bell, the site of the largest prehistoric hill fort in Northumberland. A mighty stone rampart enclosing an area of 5 hectares (12 acres) surrounds the fort. Inside the fort traces of up to 130 hut circles have been found. The views encountered on the walk are full of beauty and interest, giving the walker a day to remember.

➻ Walk through the village, heading west, and cross a road bridge spanning the College Burn. Immediately after the bridge, turn left to cross a step stile in a stone wall. Pass through a wooded area. After the trees, continue along beside a wire fence to your right until you come to a stile. Cross the stile and turn left. On coming to a ladder stile in a stone wall, cross over and go down a short, steep slope. Turn right at the bottom and follow wooden marker posts with the College Burn on your left.

College Burn derives its name from two old Saxon words 'col' and 'leche', meaning a stream flowing through boggy land. Due to its close proximity to the border, the village of Kirknewton suffered badly from Scottish raids between the 14th and 16th centuries.

➻ At the next gate, pass through and over rock-strewn ground dotted with gorse bushes. On reaching a path leading up a steep slope to your right, climb the slope. At the top turn left. Keep near a wire fence to your left till you come to a stile. Cross the stile and turn right to contour the slopes of Hethpool Bell, crossing stiles when you encounter them. The path drops down to join another above the College Burn.

Hethpool Bell is covered in oak trees reputed to have been planted by the famous Admiral Lord Collingwood in the 19th century. The National Park have been planting new oaks to replace some of the older ones. Roe deer inhabit the wood and are best seen at dusk or early morning when they leave the security of the trees to forage for food.

↳ Turn left and go down a short slope to a gated footbridge spanning the College Burn. Cross the bridge and close the gate behind you. A path climbs to your left, through trees, to a wire fence. Cross via a stile and turn right to climb out of the valley. At the top follow the path, with a wire fence to your right and a deep, tree-clad gully to your left. On coming to a marker post, turn half left and down into a small, shallow gully. Ford a narrow stream at its base before climbing up the other side.

Take care coming out of the gully as the path is lined with gorse, the thorns of which are very sharp.

↳ The path leads to a wire fence crossed by a stile. Bear half left and pass to the right of a sheep fold. Pass a marker post and keep ahead as directed to a track, which is a permissive way. Turn left and follow the track up the slope to a plantation of coniferous trees. Go through the trees and exit the other side. Walk to the right of the buildings of Kirknewton Tor, marked on some maps as Torleehouses, to join a good farm road. Remain on the road till you reach a marker post before a cattle grid. Turn right, as directed by a yellow arrow, on to a track running parallel to a stone wall. The track rises to a gate that you go through.

To the side of the gate is a notice: 'Please take care. Some of the ground nesting birds that breed here during the spring are easily disturbed by people, and more so by dogs. During April, May and June you can help minimise such disturbances by keeping dogs on a lead and keeping to the paths.'.

↳ The path bends left and then right, climbing a steep grass slope with a stone wall to the left. Keep close to the wall and climb to a stile. Cross the wall at this point. A broad track curves right, taking you along the top of a valley dropping away to the left.

The majestic hill across the valley is Yeavering Bell, your ultimate destination. On the slopes of the hill the observant walker may see some of the wild goats which roam the area. They are not really wild in the true sense but are feral. They are probably descended from goats kept for milk, perhaps from as far back as Roman times.

↳ Stay on the track until you reach a low signpost on your left. Turn left, as directed for Yeavering Bell and Gleadscleugh, and descend into the valley. At

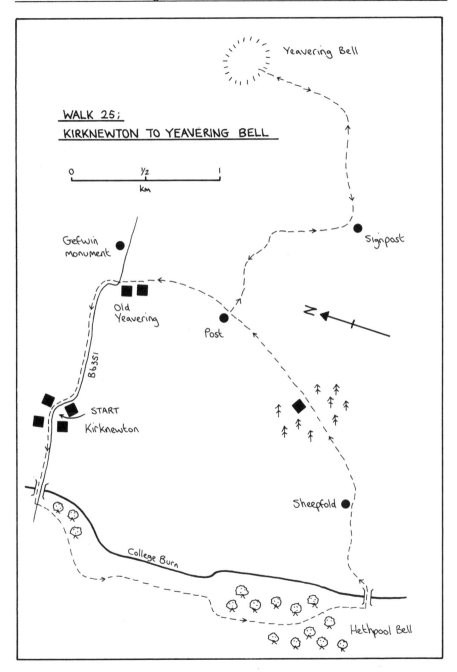

WALK 25;
KIRKNEWTON TO YEAVERING BELL

0   ½   1
         km

Yeavering Bell

Gefwin Monument

Signpost

Old Yeavering

Post

B6351

N

START
Kirknewton

Sheepfold

College Burn

Hethpool Bell

Summit cairn and view east from Yeavering Bell

the foot, ford a narrow stream and climb to a marker post. Pass through bracken before coming to another marker post. Climb the slope of Yeavering Bell with further marker posts guiding you along. As you climb, pass through what seems to have been an ancient stone enclosure. At the last marker post turn half right and climb the last bit to a gap in the ramparts. It is through here you have access to the fort.

From the summit there are excellent views overlooking the surrounding countryside. Despite its low height, the view equals some of the best obtained from higher hills within the Cheviots.

↳ After your exploration of the site, return to the gap in the ramparts and retrace your steps down the hill and across the valley to the low signpost. Turn right and back down the track to the farm road from Kirknewton Tor. Once on the farm road, turn right and cross the cattle grid to pass through a wall. Remain on the track and go over the next cattle grid. The track descends gently to a gate, which you go through. Cross a narrow stream before coming to the next gate. Pass through the gate and along the side of the cottages of Old Yeavering to a surfaced road. Turn left to follow the road back to your starting point.

Local Attractions

The church of St Gregory in Kirknewton is mentioned in records dating from the 12th century. In the latter part of the 15th century the church was rebuilt after falling derelict. Further rebuilding was undertaken in 1669, and again in 1856. Inside the church is a curious sculpture of the Virgin Mary and the Magi in which the Magi are depicted wearing what appears to be kilts. The graveyard contains the grave of Josephine Butler, a famous Victorian social reformer for women, who died in 1906.

26. low steaos to howick hall

Distance: 5½ miles, 8.5km
Grade: Medium
Maps: Ordnance Survey Landranger 81, Pathfinder 477 NU21/22
Refreshments: Alnwick (5½ miles) for pubs, cafés, hotels and restaurants.
Start: Cliff top parking area after Low Steads Farm. GR263156

This coastal walk is so full of interest that it could stretch to fill your day. Beginning with a bracing walk along the dramatic Northumbrian coastline, you then turn inland to visit the gardens of Howick Hall. These gardens, beautiful and full of interest, are truly spectacular early in the year when they are alight with spring bulbs. The walk returns along a privately owned woodland path to the coast, and then back to your starting point.

♴ Turn north from the parking area and follow a broad track along the top of the cliffs. There will be a wire fence and fields to your left. After 750 metres the track descends a short slope to a gate. Pass through the gate and cross a narrow, concrete footbridge spanning the Howick Burn.

This section is delightful, taking in fine views of the coastline above the secluded sandy bays of Howdiement Sands and Sugar Sands.

♴ Once across the bridge, proceed straight ahead to pass through a gate set in a stone wall. A dozen paces later you pass through another gate. The track continues with a wire fence to your right. After passing a wooden gate set in the fence to your right, you will come to a fence across your way. Go through the gate to pastureland. At the next gate use the stile to the right. Ahead you will see a single row of houses known as Seahouses.

Not be confused with the larger seaside resort of Seahouses further up the coast.

♴ The track progresses to the left of Seahouses and through a gate. The track joins a surfaced road.

For walkers who would like a pleasant diversion to a secluded bay, I can highly recommend the following. Continue along the road for ninety metres, to a gate in the fence to your right. Pass through the gate and along a grassy path to another gate. Once through this gate turn half-right to reach a delightful bay.

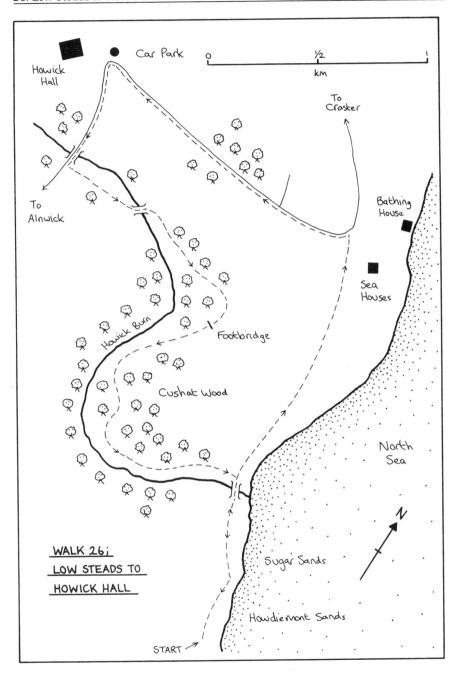

Howick Hall

● Car Park

0   ½   1
km

To Craster

Howick Hall

To Alnwick

Bathing House

Sea Houses

Footbridge

Howick Burn

Cushat Wood

North Sea

N

WALK 26;
LOW STEADS TO
HOWICK HALL

Sugar Sands

Howdiemont Sands

START →

✤ To continue on the original walk, turn left and follow the road for 800 metres to reach the entrance to Howick Hall.

The hall was built in 1782 for the Grey family and has extensive grounds. The gardens are open to the public and are well worth visiting. In spring the gardens are strewn with daffodils, whilst later in the season the beds of rhododendrons provide a blaze of colour to delight the eye. Howick Hall was the home of the great reformer Earl Grey, who attempted to stamp out corruption in politics. He is probably better known to tea enthusiasts for the brand of tea that bears his name.

✤ If you are not visiting the hall, follow the road as it bends left and passes under a narrow footbridge. Cross the road bridge spanning the Howick Burn. Immediately at the end of the bridge, turn left and go through a revolving gate in a high, wire mesh fence. A grassy path takes you to a small footbridge across the Howick Burn. Once over you come to a fork. Do not take the fork to the left as this leads into private grounds. Take the track to the right where, after a few paces, you pass a stone pillar.

This pillar bears a plaque which reads: 'The Long Walk. These woods are privately owned and there is no public right of way. However, members of the public are very welcome to walk in them at their own risk since there are many old trees. Please keep to the path, keep your dogs on leads at all times, do not pick the flowers – they are there for the enjoyment of all. Do not carve on or otherwise damage the trees. The Long Walk will be closed every second Wednesday of every February. By order Howick Trustees LTD. I hope walkers follow this good advice.

✤ The track meanders through the trees, shrubs and new plantings. In autumn the track is a golden carpet of leaves, whilst the display of spring flowers early in the year is famous throughout the area. At a fork in the track take the stronger track to the right. This curves to the right through trees to another diversion of the track. Here we take the track to the left. To your right flows the Howick Burn.

Walking through these woods, I have often seen red squirrels clambering among the branches of the mature beech trees. Howick Estates would appreciate being informed if walkers spot any grey squirrel within their estate. Please ring the estate office and inform them of the location of the sighting. Telephone 01665 577285 as soon as possible.

✤ On coming to a high, wire mesh fence across the way, go through a revolving metal gate. Once through the gate follow the path, with beds of wild rhubarb to the right.

Wild rhubarb is highly poisonous and should not be touched. All parts of the plant are dangerous, unlike the stems of its cultivated relative.

Along the coastal path

✎ The path then passes through an area underplanted with rhododendrons.

The rhododendron is not a native plant to this country. It was brought in from the Far East during Victorian times. As well as being planted for decorative purposes, it is also planted as a cover for game birds.

✎ Remain on the path to emerge on the seashore. Turn right and cross the concrete footbridge crossed earlier in the walk. After passing through a gate, follow the track along the cliff top to return to your starting point.

Local Attractions

Howick Hall's fine gardens are open to the public and are well worth a visit. An admission fee is charged. The gardens, with their colourful displays, are a delight in the spring and autumn and there is a woodland walk to enjoy. Enquiries and opening times, telephone 01665 577285.

27. milfielð to crookhouses

Distance: 6 miles, 9.5km

Grade: Medium

Maps: Ordnance Survey Landranger 75, Pathfinder 463 NT83/93

Refreshments: In Milfield, the Milfield Country Café specialises in fine food and home-made meals. The café also contains a well-stocked craft shop and an interesting archaeological display, and is a National Park local information centre.

Start: Opposite the Crookhouses signpost just after Milfield playing field, at the side of the road to Lanton Farm. Park carefully. GR934336

On this walk we travel from Milfield up Coldside Hill to view the whole of this interesting area. From its summit, a fine view of the Cheviot Hills is reward in itself for the climb. A farm track and quiet country lanes return you to Milfield. Milfield is a small village boasting a village shop and post office, a café, a pub, the village school and a church. Milfield has a long history. It was once the royal city of the Saxon kings of Northumbria, with the palace located on the outskirts of the present village. Recent excavations have produced some interesting finds, including the remains of a hinge. During the Border troubles Milfield frequently suffered attacks by Scottish raiding parties and today little remains of the original village. During the Second World War Milfield again gained prominence when RAF Milfield came into existence. The airfield was constructed to the south of the village. Initially used to train British pilots, it was later utilised by the Americans and was operational until 1946. In 1966 a private flying club took over the airfield. In 1984 they purchased an adjacent farm at Galewood and transferred to new premises there. Due to quarrying operations, little now remains of the original airfield, apart from a short stretch of runway and some ruinous buildings.

↳ Proceed up the rising track signposted for Crookhouses. As you progress higher up the hillside, the view to your left opens out with views of the Milfield Plain and the Cheviots. Pass through a gate across the track. Continue ahead, keeping a stone wall to your left. At the next gate, once again pass through, walking along the right-hand side of a small plantation of coniferous

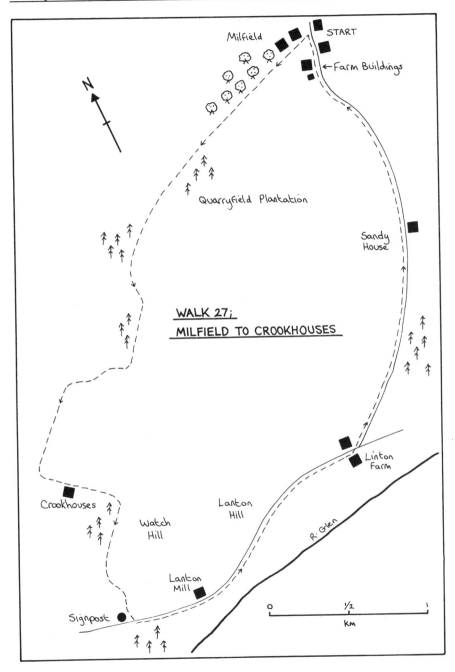

Milfield

START

←Farm Buildings

N

Quarryfield Plantation

Sandy House

WALK 27;
MILFIELD TO CROOKHOUSES

Linton Farm

Crookhouses

Lanton Hill

Watch Hill

R. Glen

Lanton Mill

Signpost

0   ½   1
km

Looking back on the track ascending the eastern side of Coldside Hill

trees. Once past the plantation, keep on the track to go along the left side of another plantation.

Here you have fine views of the countryside to the south as well as the Milfield Plain. The land to the east of Milfield was once a vast lake. The lake was created at the end of the last Ice Age from melt water running from the retreating glaciers. Neolithic man settled on the edge of the lake to fish and gather food, later setting up an agricultural base in scattered settlements across the plain. Minerals deposited from the lake gave fine, enriched soil for cultivation and the growing of crops.

✤ At the end of the trees the path bends sharp right to a gate. At this point do not turn right, instead walk straight ahead over grass to pass through another gate. Follow a grassy path, with a broken stone wall to your left. Keep near the wall and where it curves left, follow to reach a gate. This gate bears a yellow marker arrow. Go through the gate and turn right to walk parallel to a stone wall. Ahead is a plantation; to your left are open fields. Walk along the left edge of the plantation.

Looking left you can see an obelisk on the top of Lanton Hill. Sir William Davison of Lanton erected the obelisk in memory of his father, Alexander Davison, and his brother, John Davison.

꙳ After the plantation, the path makes a slight descent to two gates. Ignore the one in the wall and pass through the one ahead which bears a yellow arrow. The path follows beside a stone wall to your right. On coming to a gate in the wall, pass through the gate. Proceed along with the wall to your right until you reach a farm track and a marker post. Turn left and descend towards the buildings of Crookhouses. After passing through gates, walk along the side of Crookhouses to a narrow, surfaced road. Keep to the road as it contours the hillside and descends to a signpost.

The signpost bears directions to West Newton, Crookhouses and Flodden.

꙳ Turn left at the signpost and past the cottage of Lanton Mill. Remain on the road with a stone wall to your left.

Looking up to your left you can see the Davison obelisk on top of Lanton Hill. In September the sides of the road are lined with blackberry bushes that provide a tasty nibble. The River Glen flows to your right.

꙳ At the farm buildings of Lanton, pass through. Just prior to the last building there is a road leading off to the left. Turn left and go along this road for 1½ miles to return to your starting point.

28. mounthooly to ounsoale

Distance: 4 miles, 6.4 km

Grade: Medium

Maps: Ordnance Survey Landrangers 74, Pathfinder 474 NT82/92, Outdoor Leisure 16

Refreshments: Wooler (10 miles) – cafés, pubs and hotels. Milfield (11 miles) – Milfield Country Café.

Start: At the last gate before Mounthooly. GR882227

Mounthooly is set in the attractive College Valley, an excellent location for walking on good paths in varied countryside with many features of interest for family walks. This walk is an ideal introduction to this attractive area.

✤ Pass through the gate. At a fork just before the white bungalow of Mounthooly, take the track to the right which leads behind the bungalow.

The older house beside the bungalow is a bunkhouse converted from the former shepherd's farmhouse. The bunkhouse can cater for single walkers and groups of up to 25. Telephone 01668 216358 for further details and bookings.

✤ Once past Mounthooly, the track travels along the bottom of a conifer plantation to open grassland. If you look behind the sheep pens to your right, you can pick out the remains of a Bronze Age burial site. At a wire fence across the track, go through the gate.

The area to the right after the gate is planted with broad-leaved trees. These were planted in 1995. Thirty-five hectares of forestry were felled to enable the planting of 70 hectares of native broad-leaved trees. This project hopes to recreate the natural vegetation of the area. The scheme was grant-aided by Northumberland National Park and the Forestry Authority.

✤ After passing through the gate, walk on 25 metres to a marker post. Turn left down the bank to the College Burn. Ford the burn, climb up the other side and pass to the left of a sheepfold.

Sheepfolds are known locally as stells, and are still in use today by shepherds during the lambing season.

✤ After 50 metres turn left at a wooden post to ford the narrow Braydon Burn,

Looking east along the Lambden Valley

calm in summer but turbulent after autumn rains or winter thaws. Continue along the flank of Cheviot on a path rising towards the top right corner of the conifer plantation. Before you get to the corner of the trees, climb a ladder stile over a high deer fence.

The fence is here to protect newly planted trees within the enclosure from damage by deer, sheep and feral goats.

↳ Ignore a gate to your right and cross a second, smaller stile leading into the trees. A narrow path threads through the trees for 300 metres before bending right to a wire fence. Walk beside the fence with the plantation to your left and open ground to your right. Pass an old metal shed, formerly used for the storage of winter sheep fodder, before coming to a stile in the fence marked with a yellow arrow. Cross this stile and bear half left across rough ground, aiming for the right-hand side of a plantation seen ahead.

Mountain birds such as grouse, wheatear, golden plover and dotteral may be seen on the peat moors in the area. Underfoot you will see heather, ling, cotton grass, bilberry and cloudberry. Behind the trees rises Coldburn Hill. As you approach the corner of the plantation, looking left through the gap you can see Newton Tors.

↳ At the fence, cross the stile and turn first right, and then left, to walk parallel to the side of the trees with a wire fence and open ground to your right. As you progress the path begins to descend into the Lambden Valley, curving to the right. On reaching a stile in the fence, cross over. Turn left and continue to descend.

At a gap in the trees where the overhead electricity lines pass through, admire the view before you. The burn meanders along the flood plain of the valley with Coldburn and Southernknowe cottages above. Behind them rises Blackhaggs Rig, and to the right the tree-clad Loft Hill.

ᴪ At the foot of the descent is a marker post. Ahead and to your right stands the white-painted house of Dunsdale.

In December 1944, during a late afternoon blizzard, a flying fortress of the United States Army Air Force crashed into the Cheviot. Local shepherds, John Dagg who lived at Dunsdale, accompanied by his collie dog Sheila, and Frank Moscop from nearby Southernknowe, heard the explosion of the crash and set out to investigate. The dog Sheila found four airmen sheltering in a peat hole. Another three airmen found their way down to Mounthooly, the remaining two airmen were killed in the crash. As a result of their actions, both shepherds received the BEM. Sheila the collie received the Dickens Medal, the animal equivalent to the VC.

ᴪ Turn left at the post and into the trees. After a short distance emerge on open hillside with a wire fence to your right. Below you flows the Lambden Burn, above which towers the impressive rock-strewn side of Coldburn Hill. On coming to a stile in the fence, cross over and turn left. Keep the wire fence to your left and a steep drop to your right. Cross a heather-clad gully, and at the next stile recross the fence. Turn right through bracken and heather, keeping near to the fence which is now on your right.

Bracken is the enemy of farmers and shepherds. It contains numerous poisons to deter grazing animals. Over the past few years it has spread in epidemic proportions across parts of north Northumberland. The fronds stifle and crowd out most other plants and grass, taking over the land and making it unsuitable for anything.

ᴪ At the next stile, climb back over the fence and bear half right as directed by a yellow arrow. The path descends towards the valley floor. At a point where the path bends sharply right, take a lesser path leading off left. Climb a short slope then go left along the side of a gully. Descend into the gully to cross a stream at the bottom, and climb out keeping parallel to the fence on your left. Pass by and ignore a gate in the fence. At the stile cross the fence

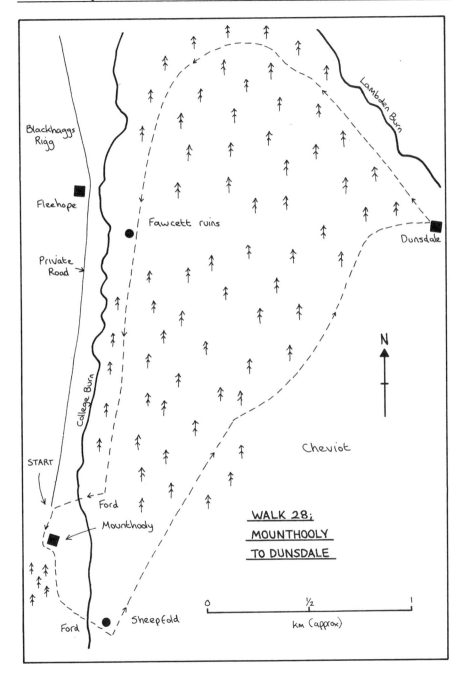

Blackhaggs Rigg

Fleehope

Fawcett ruins

Private Road →

College Burn

Lambden Burn

Dunsdale

START

Ford

Mounthooly

Cheviot

N

Ford

Sheepfold

WALK 28;
MOUNTHOOLY
TO DUNSDALE

0 ½ 1

km (approx)

and bear right as directed by the yellow arrow. The path is indistinct as it passes through an area of felled trees. Keep within sight of the wire fence to your right until you reach a point where it drops to the valley floor. Turn left into the trees. A path rises to the right before contouring the hill and turning left up an incline to a forest road. Turn right and down the road.

As you walk along you can see the cottage and gardens of Coldburn below to the right.

♭ On reaching a marker post to the left of the road, turn left up the steep bank. At the top turn half right through trees. The path gradually bears left, crossing a firebreak, to another marker post. Continue straight ahead to cross a broad forestry road to a marker post. Turn half left down through the trees to a wire fence. Cross via the stile to open ground. Turn left along the side of the trees, parallel to the wire fence. To your right are the farm buildings of Fleahope whilst below you flows the College Burn. On coming to a fence across your way, pass through the gate, keeping next to the wire fence on your left. Pass and ignore a gate leading into the trees.

To your right, at the foot of the slope, are the remains of the old farmstead of Fawcett Shank. Only earthworks remain to mark the spot where it once stood but its layout is clearly visible.

♭ At the end of the field look for and cross a stile leading into the plantation which bulges out at this point. A narrow path takes you through the trees before curving left up a steep bank to a forestry road. Turn right and follow the road until you come to a marker post. Again turn right, but this time descend through the trees to the eroded banks of the College Burn. Ford across as best you can.

This could be difficult after wet weather. The Cheviot streams are always icy cold, beginning as they do high up as mountain springs.

♭ Once across the burn, bear left to a wire fence, turn right and walk adjacent to the fence, up the field margin to cross a stile and return to your starting point.

29. ɴoʀɦaɱ to ɦoʀɴcliꝺꝺe

Distance: 5½ miles, 8.8km

Grade: Easy

Maps: Ordnance Survey Landranger 75, Pathfinder 451 NT84/94

Refreshments: Norham – pubs and hotels, Horncliffe – The Fishers Arms. Salutation Inn is 2 miles away on the A695 to Berwick. Berwick upon Tweed (7 miles) – numerous pubs, hotels and cafés.

Start: At the east end of Norham village. Roadside parking. GR 474474

This walk begins and ends in the peaceful, rural village of Norham. This quiet village has had a turbulent past due to its close proximity to the Scottish border. Named for its position next to a safe fording point of the River Tweed, in Saxon times it was known as Ubban-ford. In 1080 it became known as Norham, and was regarded as the capital of Norhamshire. The village was razed to the ground twice by Scottish raiding parties, once in 1136 and again in 1356. The present church of St Cuthbert in Norham is well worth a visit. It was built on the site of an earlier church dating from AD830. This older church housed the bones of St Ceolwule, a former king of Northumbria, to whom Bede dedicated his famous history. Overlooking the village stand the ruins of Norham Castle. The castle was built on the order of the Prince Bishop of Durham, Bishop Flambard, in 1121. It pro-tected this part of the county palatine of Durham and safeguarded the ford across the Tweed. Our walk travels from Norham to Horn-cliffe across agricultural land and returns along the wooded banks of the Tweed, where wildlife is abundant and glimpses of the salmon fishermen fascinating. It is a beautiful walk – on a summer's day, take a picnic and make a day of it.

ॐ From your starting point, walk up the road leading from Norham to Norham Castle. Just prior to the castle go through a gate in the stone wall to your left. A path takes you down a slight slope and bends right to pass along the edge of trees to a stile. Cross over the stile. To your left flows the River Tweed.

The Tweed is internationally famous for its salmon and trout fishing. River trout, unlike sea trout, spend all their lives in freshwater lakes and rivers. They average from 80 and 100 cms (about 3ft) in length, and

Norham Castle

weigh up to 10 to 15kgs (about 28lbs) when mature. The Tweed is the longest river in the region, with a length of 94 miles (156 km). It runs eastwards from the Tweedsmuir Hills in Scotland and into the North Sea at Berwick upon Tweed.

✧ A path takes you along a tree-clad slope with high crags to your right. Cross a narrow gorge using the wooden footbridge provided. Turn right as indicated by a wooden marker post immediately adjacent to it. Climb through the trees on a narrow path to emerge at a wire fence crossed by a stile. Once over, turn half left as indicated by a yellow marker arrow. Proceed along a field margin with trees and a hedge to your left.

The open land to your right is Hangman's Land. In 1513 James IV besieged Norham Castle. A story recalls that a traitorous groom from the castle advised James to concentrate his attack on a certain weak spot in the castle walls. Consequently, the castle fell. As a reward for his treachery the groom was hanged in this field the following day.

✧ The path curves left, following the field edge. At the top corner of the field is a stile in the wire fence to your left. Cross the stile and turn right to follow an indistinct path through trees and undergrowth. Keep the fence visible to your right and you cannot go wrong. At a wooden fence across the path, cross the

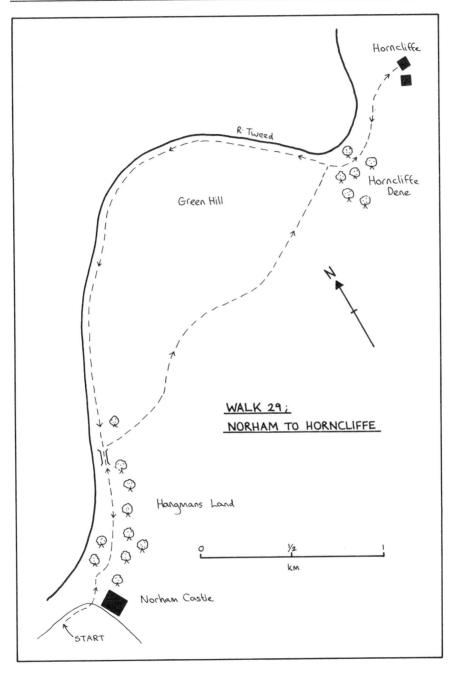

stile, and after 30 metres cross the next fence by another stile. Turn left along a field margin with trees to your left.

Hedges are the home of mice, shrews, hedgehogs, stoats and rabbits. During the 1950s a disease known as myxomatosis decimated the rabbit population of Britain. Since then the rabbit population has steadily grown and recovered its pre-myxomatosis numbers.

℞ On coming to the end of the trees, the path curves right with a wire fence to your left. Later the path bends right and then left again. Just prior to this last bend is a hawthorn tree. Behind the tree is a stile.

This stile is not easy to see from the field edge because of its position behind the tree. So keep your eyes open at this point.

℞ Once over the stile, turn right and walk along the edge of another field. At the top corner cross a stile to a farm road.

This farm road allows fishermen vehicular access to the banks of the River Tweed.

℞ Cross the road to a stile and wooden marker post bearing a yellow arrow. After crossing the stile, walk straight ahead over a field, aiming for the next marker post. This is located at the opposite side of the field in a gap in the boundary hedge. On reaching the post, cross the stile next to it and turn half left as directed by the yellow arrow. Walk across the field, aiming this time for the rooftops of Horncliffe visible above trees ahead. The path leads to a gate in a wire fence. Do not go through the gate. Turn right and go down the field margin to a stile leading into a tree-clad dene.

Walkers will frequently encounter stiles or marker posts bearing yellow arrows. These indicate the direction of a public footpath. A public footpath is a statutory right of way to which the public has access at all times. If fields are cultivated or ploughed this does not affect your rights, provided you keep to the statutory right of way at all times. Blue arrows indicate a public bridleway, also a statutory right of way.

℞ Cross the stile and turn half right through trees and up a slight slope to a fence. Turn left and walk parallel to the fence to a hawthorn hedge. Turn left and then follow the hedge as it bends to the right. Continue beside the hedge until you reach a stile at the end.

Looking down to your left you can see the River Tweed. Ahead of you the roof tops of the village of Horncliffe are visible.

℞ Cross the stile and turn left along a field edge. To your left is a wire fence with trees behind. On coming to a stile set in the fence, cross on to a well-defined path. Turn right and follow the path through trees. Where the trees end, the path continues along the top of a steep slope that drops away to your left. The path then enters more trees and comes to a signpost bearing directions for Horncliffe. Turn left and descend the steps into a deep gorge.

This gorge is Horncliffe Dene, a favourite spot for local botanists. The steep, tree-clad sides are covered in honeysuckle, gorse and ivy.

↳ Cross a wooden footbridge at the bottom of the gorge and remain on the path as it winds through trees and into Horncliffe.

Horncliffe is a quiet village with only one pub, the Fishers Arms. Charles I and Oliver Cromwell and their armies passed through the village to ford the Tweed. About half a mile to the east of Horncliffe is a honey farm that is open to the public.

↳ Return to the bridge in Horncliffe Dene and climb the steps to the signpost. Turn right and follow the path. You come to a stile on your left which you crossed earlier, do not cross it again. Pass by and follow the path through the trees to emerge on open land at the top of a slope. The path drops towards the bank of the Tweed. The last stage of the descent is eased using steps cut in the hillside. Cross a stile at the foot of the steps, and turn half left to cross another stile, which allows you access to the riverbank. Turn left and follow the bank.

Across the river can be seen a small, ruined building. You will see quite a few of these along the banks of the Tweed. These small buildings are used by fishermen and called shiels. Some are in ruins but others have been renovated and are in use.

↳ Walk along the riverbank and pass to the right of a ruined shiel. The path continues with a field to your left. On joining a broad track, you pass around another shiel. This one is in current use. Continue along the riverbank.

Stretches of riverbank are infested with giant hogweed. Despite attempts to eradicate this plant, it continues to thrive and spread. Beware of touching this plant as the sap can cause serious blistering to skin when exposed to sunlight.

↳ After passing a stone and earth jetty the path goes through a broad patch of giant hogweed before entering the wooded slope of the riverbank.

The walk along the bank through the trees has been prepared and maintained to encourage walkers. Bridges and steps help over difficult sections.

↳ The path eventually leaves the trees via a stile set in a fence. A grassy path takes you in a curve to the left and climbs a short slope to the surfaced road leading into Norham. Turn right and down the road to return to your starting point. However, if you wish, you can turn left to end your walk by visiting the ruins of Norham Castle.

Norham Castle is featured in Sir Walter Scott's *Marmion*.

Local Attractions

Norham Castle ruins are open to the public. The castle is managed by English Heritage and admission is free. Enquiries and opening times, telephone 01289 382329.

Chain Bridge Honey Farm is located about half a mile to the east of Horncliffe. Visitors can find out how bees make honey and learn about the amazing bee dance. Special observation hives allow you to look inside and watch the world of the honeybee. In the visitor's shop you can buy from a wide range of products made from beeswax, honey and propolis produced on the farm. Enquiries and opening times, telephone 01289 386362.

Norham Station Museum stands on the old railway line between Kelso and Berwick. The museum contains a model railway, a working signal box, and a varied collection of railway artefacts. Tel: 01289-382217.

30. Old Bewick to Blawearie

Distance: 4 miles, 6.5km

Grade: Medium

Maps: Ordnance Survey Landranger 75, Pathfinder 476 NU02/12

Refreshments: Eglingham (3 miles) – The Tankerville Arms, Chatton (4½ miles) – The Percy Arms, Alnwick (10 miles) – numerous pubs, cafés and restaurants.

Start: Grass verges opposite Old Bewick Cottages. GR066215

Here is a walk that travels to visit artefacts from the very dawn of history before pausing at a lonely moorland cottage. It finishes with an airy hill walk and examines ancient carvings. We start at Old Bewick, a village with a few cottages, a telephone box and the usual farm buildings. A good track ascends to an impressive, ancient burial site containing four burial chambers. Its isolated position on this windswept moor is evocative enough, but its close proximity to many mysterious carved rocks and a Bronze Age fort has enormous power to conjure up visions of our ancestors who lived and died in these hills. We continue to Blawearie, but pause to consider the patience of a shepherd who created a garden carved from the hillside to enhance his lonely cottage before we stride over Bewick Hill to admire the stunning views. To the south of Old Bewick flows the River Breamish, which changes its name to Till at Bewick Bridge. An old couplet states,

'Foot of Breamish and head of Till
Meet together at Bewick Mill.'

This walk is at its best in spring or late autumn. In high summer the bracken hides many of its finer points.

↬ From the parking area, ascend the cobbled track from Old Bewick Cottages and pass through a metal gate. The track climbs gently, bending to the left.

> Where the track bends left there is a low bank and trees to your right. Behind them are the remains of an old reservoir. Bewick is believed to have originated from an old English word 'beswic', meaning 'bee farm'.

↬ The track heads to a stone wall skirting the lower slopes of Bewick Hill.

Pass through a gate in the wall and walk on with a stone wall to your left. Ignore the gate in this wall, and after 35 metres go through a gate across the track. When the track forks, take the left fork and go on to another gate. Go through a kissing gate to the left of the main gate. A dirt track takes you to the next fork where you take the right fork. The track then climbs a short rise and the ruins of the shepherd's cottage of Blawearie become visible ahead. Make your way towards them.

Just subsequent to Blawearie and off to the left of the track is a stone-walled enclosure. This is worth a visit as it is a prehistoric burial site. The site is around 3500 years old. A large stone enclosure encircles the burial ground in which cists can be seen. A cist was a burial chamber. It was constructed by using four large stone slabs to form an oblong or square shape for the sides. A larger stone known as the capstone is placed on top as a lid. The dead were curled up in the foetal position and placed in the cist. Buried alongside the body would be items for use in the afterlife. Flint knives and bead necklaces have been found. A cist could also contain cremated remains placed in an urn. Many artefacts found at this site are displayed at the Museum of Archaeology at Newcastle upon Tyne.

⤷ At Blawearie, take time to explore the area and absorb the solitude. To the east of the cottage is a garden created amidst crags.

This former shepherd's cottage was built in the 19th century and occupied up to the start of the Second World War. The army then used it before it was abandoned and left to fall into ruin. To the eastern side of the cottage, set amidst crags, are the remains of a well-cared for and loved garden. Flower beds are carefully laid out amongst the crags. As you enter the garden, a flight of steps cut into stone crag to your left allows you access to further flower terraces.

⤷ From Blawearie, retrace your steps for about 45 metres to a wooden marker post to the side of the track. Leave the track and turn left as indicated to follow a grassy path through bracken. Pass a marker post and continue on a well-defined path that bends to the left. To your right, on top of a small hillock, is a stone cairn. Keep to the path until you reach a fork. Take the right fork and walk on for 20 metres to pass to the right of a small stone cairn. At the next stone cairn the path bends half right and proceeds through dense bracken while slowly losing height.

Looking to the left you will see the waterfall of Corby Crags. There is a

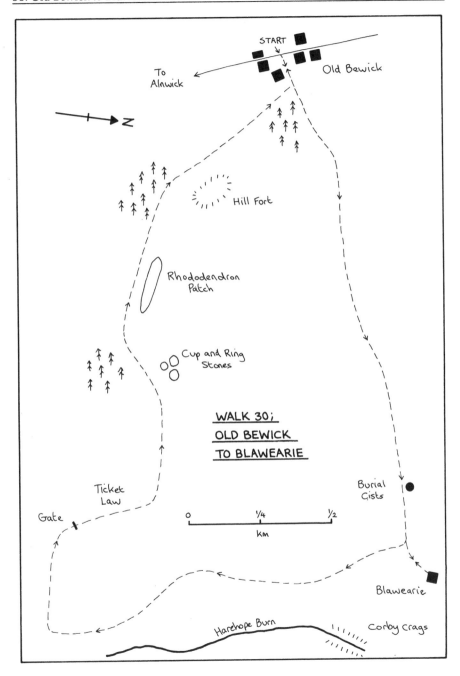

START

To
Alnwick

Old Bewick

N

Hill Fort

Rhododendron
Patch

Cup and Ring
Stones

WALK 30;
OLD BEWICK
TO BLAWEARIE

Tickek
Law

Gate

Burial
Cists

0   ¼   ½
km

Blawearie

Harehope Burn

Corby Crags

large hill fort between the path and the crags, but this is sometimes hard to discern due to the dense bracken that covers the area.

✎ At the foot of the descent cross a boggy area, aiming for a gate in the wire fence ahead. Prior to reaching the gate, turn right on to a lesser path that climbs parallel to a fence on your left. Follow this path to a fence corner, where you turn right to arrive at a gate. Do not go through this gate.

Here a panoramic view emerges. Open country stretches out below and the Cheviot Hills march across the skyline to your right.

✎ Turn away from the gate and follow a track as it climbs towards the top of Bewick Hill. When the wire fence on your left bends away left, follow beside it until you come to a stone wall. Go through a wicket gate and walk half right towards a stile in a wire fence. A few paces over the stile there stands a large, square-shaped rock.

The surface of the rock is adorned with cup and ring marks. They have puzzled archaeologists for many years. These intricate designs were carved into the rock around 3000BC. The incisions were made by chiselling the soft rock with a harder stone. The meaning of these marks is lost in the mists of time, and there have been many theories put forward as to their purpose. These range from religious rituals to maps or just

Cup and Ring stone

plain doodles to pass the time. It is doubtful if we will ever know their true meaning.

↳ Return to the wicket gate in the stone wall but do not go through it. Turn right and follow a path that descends through bracken. On nearing the bottom, bear half right to join a broad track. Pass below a large planting of rhododendrons growing on the hillside to your right. Remain on the track as it leads along the side of a plantation to a gate. Once through the gate, turn half right and go up a short, steep slope. Turn left at the top and walk along a path contouring the hill. There will be a wire fence to your right. On meeting a broad, cobbled track, turn left to return to your starting point.

31. Rothbury to Lordenshaws

Distance: 5½ miles, 8.8km

Grade: Medium

Maps: Ordnance Survey Landranger 81, Pathfinders 511 NU00/10 and 500 NZ09/19

Refreshments: Rothbury has cafés, pubs and hotels.

Start: Car park on the south side of the River Coquet at Rothbury. GR056015

The cup and ring marks at Lordenshaws date from around 3000BC. The various intricate designs were partially chiselled out using Bronze Age implements. We may never know why these designs were made. As the majority have been found near burial sites, it is probable that they have some ritual significance. To the east of the markings is a hill fort dating from around 400BC. The high ramparts of the fort, whilst being a means of defence, were also a display of the wealth and power of the people who lived there. Inside the fort is the site of circular stone houses from the 1st century. To the north of the fort can be found burial cists or stone coffins which are over 3500 years old. Unfortunately, these are empty as the bodies and gifts, which would be buried with them, have long since been plundered.

↳ Cross the narrow concrete bridge spanning the River Coquet and turn left, passing a children's play area. Continue along the riverbank. Across the river you will see the green of Rothbury Golf Club. At a marker post bearing a blue arrow, keep straight ahead. Do not cross the little bridge to your left as this leads into the private grounds of the golf club. The path curves slightly right and up a bank to a signpost next to a main road. Turn left as directed and descend to a gate in a wire fence. Go through the gate.

Heron, ducks, water hen and gooseanders make their homes on the banks of the Coquet. Gooseanders were traditionally the enemy of water bailiffs because of their huge appetite for freshwater fish. Today they are a protected bird in England.

↳ At the next marker post turn left into a small gully. At the base, cross a wooden footbridge. From the bridge the path rises to a fork in the path next to an electricity pole. Take the fork right which leads to the next marker post.

Footbridge across the River Coquet at Rothbury

Below and to your left are reed beds and a wet area which is home to wild life such as frogs and reed warblers.

↳ At the post turn right to a gate. Pass through the gate to emerge on a broad farm track. Turn left and follow the track as it descends and bends left to a narrow concrete footbridge spanning the River Coquet.

This is Lady Bridge. It is thought to be so named because it provided a dry route for ladies visiting the old mills which one stood across the river. The only other route was by means of stepping stones.

↳ Once over the bridge, pass through a narrow gate and walk on a good track with a wire fence to the left, later replaced by a hedge. After 600 metres the track bends left and develops into a surfaced road as it passes the picturesque cottages of Tosson.

Tosson was once the site of a woollen mill where shepherds' plaids and fabrics were produced.

↳ At the road junction turn left. Keep on the road to pass Westnewton Farm. Soon you will arrive at Eastnewton Farm. Go through the gate in a wall to the left of the house. A signpost bears directions to Newton Park, 1 mile. A track ascends and bends left before dropping to the Black Burn. Ford the burn and immediately turn right to walk along the top of an old boundary wall. On reaching a fence, keep parallel with and close to it. At a fence across the way, cross via a stile to the right of the gate.

As the path rises take time to pause and enjoy the panoramic view of Coquetdale to your rear. Looking to the right is Rothbury.

↳ Where the fence bends left just before a stand of trees, look to your right for a marker post. Make your way to it and up a slight rise as directed by a yellow direction arrow. On coming to an old boundary wall, make for and pass through a gap to your left near to the trees. Some 30 metres on is another marker post. Pass this post and walk above a disused quarry. Keep to the field margin with a fence to your left until you reach a gate leading into a conifer plantation. Go through the gate, and a dozen paces on turn right to go through another gate. After 450 metres exit from the trees on to a narrow, surfaced road.

This is the access road to Simonside, which is beyond the cattle grid to your right.

↳ Turn left along the road, which takes you through the trees to open moorland. About 200 metres before the road enters the next plantation, you arrive at car park. Enter the car park and walk across to an information board.

This is Lordenshaws car park. The information board has a map of the site and relates the history of the hill fort and the cup and ring rocks.

↳ Walk past the information board to a marker post and continue ahead as directed. After 300 metres there is a narrow path leading off left. Take this path to view the cup and ring rock. Return to the path and walk on to a marker post bearing three sets of arrows.

If you follow the track to the right it takes you up to the hill fort.

↳ From the marker post keep straight ahead and descend the hill. At the foot of the hill turn right and go through a gate. Pass two small duck ponds and walk along the front of the cottages of Whittondean Farm. Just before the farmhouse, go through a gate to your left marked with a yellow arrow. This takes you through the farm garden to another gate. Once through this gate you emerge on a hedge-lined farm road. When you come to a junction with another farm track, turn right. Keep to the track for half a mile to pass a tall, stone-built tower.

This tower is Sharp's Folly. The Rev Dr Thomas Sharp, Rector of Rothbury from 1720 to 1758, erected it. It was built for the relief of unemployment among local stonemasons. Dr Sharp, who was a keen astronomer,

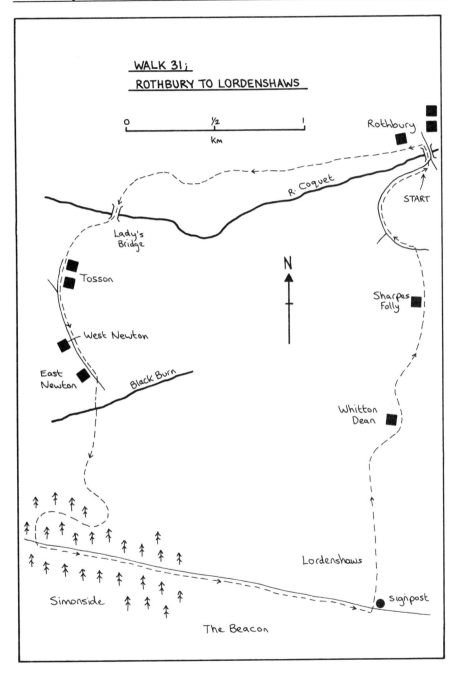

WALK 31;
ROTHBURY TO LORDENSHAWS

0   ½   1
km

Rothbury

START

R. Coquet

Lady's
Bridge

N

Tosson

Sharpes
Folly

West Newton

East
Newton

Black Burn

Whitton
Dean

Simonside

Lordenshaws

Signpost

The Beacon

used the tower as an observatory. This is the oldest folly in the county and is a listed building. From the top of the tower it was possible to see as far as the North Sea through the Coquet Gap.

꒰ At a fork in the road, take the turning to the right which leads on to a surfaced road. Turn left and follow the road downhill to a junction. This time take the right-hand turn, signposted for Rothbury, and descend to pass Rothbury Cemetery and return to your starting point at the car park.

Local Attractions

Cragside House is situated to the east of Rothbury and the house and 900-acre gardens are open to the public. The house was the home of the Victorian industrialist and inventor, Lord Armstrong. It has the distinction of being the first house in the world to be lit by hydroelectricity. This was generated in the grounds using their own water generators. The gardens and woodland walks are a treat to be enjoyed. Visitor centre and cafe. An admission fee is charged. Car parking. Enquiries and opening times, telephone 01669 620333.

32. símonsíoe cRags círcular

Distance: 5 miles, 8km

Grade: Medium, but one steep scramble uphill.

Maps: Ordnance Survey Landranger 81, Pathfinder 511 NZ09/19

Refreshments: Rothbury (3 miles) – pubs, hotels and cafés

Start: Simonside picnic area car park. GR037997

An exciting walk travelling through forest paths to open moorland. A final scramble up Simonside Crags is rewarded by unparalleled views across the northern country. The sea, the Cheviots, Coquetdale and the Tyne valley are all below you.

✎ From the picnic area, take the waymarked track designated Red Route. Pass through a gate and follow a broad forest road lined with heather, which curves to the right. Pass by a marker post and remain on the track until the track forks. At this point take the right fork.

Unlike the Cheviots, the underlying rocks on these hills are composed of sandstone, hence the presence of sand found on the paths and tracks. This makes for easy walking.

✎ Just after the fork and to the right is a tall radio mast and two sheds. When the track bends sharply to the right, leave the track for a broad path to the left bearing a marker post with a red arrow. The path climbs to pass a seat on the right.

From this seat you could once see across the countryside to the Cheviots, but over the years the trees have grown and obscured the view. However, clambering onto a large rock to the left of the path you may still enjoy the view.

✎ Continue along the path to pass a signpost for Little Church Rock.

This provides excellent views if you wish to make a slight diversion.

✎ When you reach a junction of paths, take the one to the left. This climbs through the trees. The path is badly eroded with the bedrock exposed so can be slippery after wet weather. Please take care.

Bilberry bushes grow beside the path. In late summer their edible blue berries provide a tasty snack as you pass. Collected in large amounts, these berries are also used in preserves or the making of wines and spirits. The plant favours high ground or acid moor. Wild animals also enjoy these fruits so you are very unlikely to collect enough to make wine.

✤ On leaving the trees, turn left at a marker post and cross open, heather-clad ground, making towards the ridge ahead. On coming to a broad forest road turn right.

If you feel in need of a break before the final ascent of the crags, turn left where Rothbury Forests have provided seats. You can see the River Coquet far below and to the north the Cheviot Hills march across the horizon.

✤ Where the road forks, just before a plantation, take the path to the left. After a dozen paces turn left again. The ascent now steepens as you begin to climb Simonside Crag. A short, rocky scramble brings you to the top. Turn left along the crag to a large summit cairn. Beside the cairn is a stone shelter.

I have often seen buzzards soaring gracefully around the crags. These birds hunt in open country for small mammals, insects and carrion. They have broad wings, a large, rounded tail, brown plumage and average 55cm (22ins) in length when fully grown.

✤ From the cairn, head eastwards with Old Stell Crags to your right. Marker posts guide you through heather and up to the summit of Dove Crag, where rock formations caused by erosion will arrest your progress.

The path to Dove Crag is eroded and can be boggy after rain. I remember one lady whose foot went through ice into a deep, waterlogged hole and spent the rest of the walk squelching in a water-filled boot. Red grouse inhabit the area and can be found in abundance. Their various cries as they rise noisily from the heather often startle walkers.

✤ From the summit, descend to a sign which reads Red Route Return. Ignore this sign and turn right to descend to a wire fence. Cross via a ladder stile. Follow a path which winds across heather moor to the summit of The Beacon.

From here you can see Lordenshaws hill fort with its ramparts and hut circles. Beacon Hill is so named because it was the site of a beacon that would warn of the expected invasion from the Spanish Armada.

✤ Leave The Beacon and descend with the prehistoric site of Lordenshaws visible below to your left. The path is badly eroded so take care as you descend. You will notice an old boundary wall to your right.

This wall formed part of a 13th-century deer park built by Robert

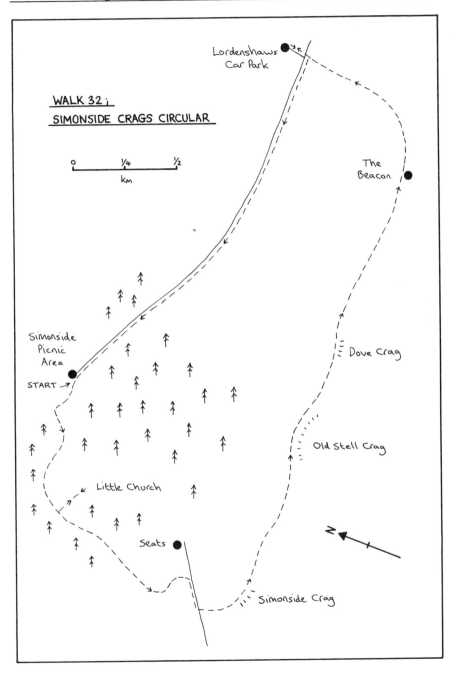

WALK 32 ;
SIMONSIDE CRAGS CIRCULAR

Lordenshaws
Car Park

The
Beacon

Simonside
Picnic
Area

START

Dove Crag

Old Stell Crag

Little Church

Seats

Simonside Crag

0   ¼   ½
km

N

FitzRoger, Lord of the Manor of Rothbury, to enable his deer to graze undisturbed. The park was abandoned towards the end of the 16th century.

↳ Keep to the path and descend to a surfaced road. If you wish to visit Lordenshaws cross the road into the car park. If not, turn left and remain on the road to cross moor before entering a plantation. The road runs through the trees and, after crossing a cattle grid, returns you to the car park and the start of the walk.

North from Dove Crag

Local Attractions

Lordenshaws is a fine prehistoric site which boasts a hill fort, burial cists and excellent examples of rock carvings. An agreement between National Parks and the Duke of Northumberland has made this area accessible to the public.

33. thrunton woods to castle hill

Distance: 4½ miles, 7.3km

Grade: Easy

Maps: Ordnance Survey Landranger 81, Pathfinders 488 NU01/11 and 500 NU00/10

Refreshments: Whittingham (3 miles) – The Castle Inn. Powburn (3½ miles) – The Plough Inn and a service station with café and restaurant, just north of Powburn on the A697, Alnwick (6 miles) – numerous pubs, restaurants and cafés.

Start: Thrunton Woods car park. GR085096

A delightful walk for all seasons, taking you on well-defined tracks and paths through woods, and culminating in a gentle climb to the summit of Castle Hill. The top of Castle Hill contains traces of ancient defensive earthworks. The walk then returns along the top of Thrunton Crags that afford excellent views of the countryside to the north. During this walk you have the opportunity of making two slight diversions to visit two caves. One was the lair of a thief; the other the retreat of a monk.

✤ Leave the parking area and turn left down the surfaced road. Ignore a forest track off to your left and continue on to where the road bends right. At this point there will be a large Rothbury Forests notice board to your left. Do not turn right to follow the road but continue straight ahead on a broad, red-stoned track. On coming to a fork, you take the stronger track to the left. After a dozen paces pass through a kissing gate and enter the woods.

The trees within these woods are mainly spruce and pine. Pine is best suited for the poor, sandy soil of the lowlands whilst spruce is ideal for the rich, peaty soil of the uplands.

✤ Follow a forest track between an avenue of trees. Pass by a marker post bearing red and orange direction arrows. The track makes a descent with open land to your right before re-entering the woods. Remain on the track until you come to a circular clearing. There will be a signpost to your left for Wedderburn Hole.

If time permits, it is worth visiting the Hole. It will probably add twenty minutes to your time. A path steeply climbs through trees and bracken.

Pass a large boulder and some smaller caves. Keep climbing to reach a signpost for Wedderburn Hole, which will located to the right of the sign. Thomas Wedderburn was a local rogue who stole sheep and cattle from the nearby farms. One day, pursued by angry farmers, he sought refuge in this cave in the hillside. The farmers found his hiding place but were unable to enter because of the narrow entrance. They dug a small hole in the top of the cave and fired a pistol through it. The bullet struck and killed Thomas. Above the cave entrance the initials 'TW' are carved in the rock. Retrace your steps back to the track.

↳ From the signpost, continue along the track to reach a path branching off to the right. There is a marker post at this point. Turn right and follow this path through the trees to emerge on open ground. Turn left and go along a red-stone track as it travels along the side of trees before curving right and entering the woods.

Forest Enterprise is part of the Forestry Commission and is responsible for the management of woodlands and forests owned by the nation. The production and supply of timber for the wood industry is one of its objectives, as is the conservation and protection of wildlife within its forests. The Commission also provides the public with a wide range of recreational activities.

↳ The track curves and meets up with another track at a marker post. Turn right, as indicated by an orange arrow. The track ascends a slope before levelling out at a junction of tracks. Look to your left and you will see an old stone wall with a gap. There will be a signpost next to the gap bearing directions for Castle Hill. Pass through the gap. A narrow path climbs through trees and bracken to bring you to the summit of Castle Hill.

The summit is topped with massive, old beech trees and surrounded by two ancient, concentric earthworks.

↳ Proceed ahead through the beech trees to a marker post bearing red and orange arrows. Turn half left and begin to descend into a deep valley. At the next marker post turn right to continue the descent, which gets steeper. On the valley floor pass another marker post and go on to a wire fence. Cross via the stile and turn half right.

After crossing the stile there will be a signpost bearing directions to Macartney's Cave. To visit the cave, climb a narrow path up the bracken-covered slope. On reaching a tall column of sandstone, the cave entrance is seen about a quarter of the way up. A narrow ledge enters it to the left of the entrance. Inside the cave it is possible for two

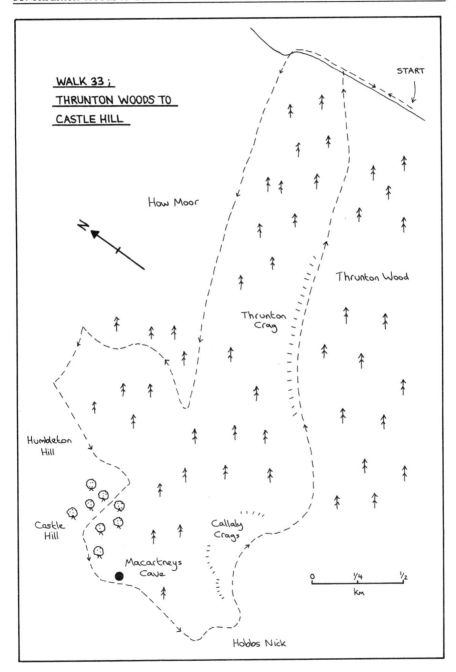

WALK 33 ;
THRUNTON WOODS TO
CASTLE HILL

START

How Moor

Thrunton Wood

Thrunton
Crag

Humbleton
Hill

Castle
Hill

Callaly
Crags

Macartneys
Cave

0   ¼   ½
km

Hobbs Nick

The monk's cave in Thrunton Wood

adults to stand. Brother Macartney, a monk who lived in Kildare, made the cave, chiselling it out by hand. Each day the monk would sit here praying to God and meditating. Retrace your steps back down to the path.

✤ The path takes you along the base of the crags to your left before bending left and climbing. At the top of the crags the path goes through trees before emerging on open land. Cross over heather moorland to pass to the left of a small lough, or lake. The path leads to a gate set in a stone wall.

To your right you have good views over moorland with the Simonside Hills on the distant skyline.

✤ Go through the gate and turn right to re-enter the woods. Keep a stone wall to your right until you join up with a broad track. Turn left and go along the track as it travels along the top of Thrunton Crags.

In gaps between the trees to your left you have many fine views of the surrounding countryside to the north stretching up to the Cheviot Hills.

✤ Keep to the track and ignore other tracks branching off to the left or right. After one and a half miles the track emerges on a surfaced road. Turn right and go along the road to return to your starting point.

34. ᴡooleꞦ to the piꞎ ᴡell

Distance: 2¼ miles, 3.5km

Grade: Easy

Maps: Ordnance Survey Landranger 75. Pathfinder 475 NT82/92, Outdoor Leisure 16

Refreshments: There are pubs, hotels and cafés in Wooler

Start: Wooler bus station GR992281

Here is your chance to visit a magical wishing well. Remember to take a bent pin to drop in the well if you want your wish granted. Although not actually in Northumberland National Park, Wooler is adjacent to it and is an excellent base for walking. The town has accommodation to suit all tastes, including a YHA hostel. Notices on the approach to Wooler announce you are entering the gateway to the Cheviots. Wooler is the centre of commerce for a large agricultural community and has long been renowned for its cattle and sheep markets.

🌡 **Leave the bus station and cross the main road to the large café opposite. Turn left and take the second road to your right. This is Cheviot Street and it climbs steeply as it takes you out of Wooler.**

To your left as you walk up Cheviot Street stands Wooler United Reformed Church. The building was constructed in 1778 for a religious organisation known as Relief. In 1847 this church joined with the United Presbyterians, and became associated with the English Presbyterian Church in 1877. The building was renovated in this year. From 1977 to the present day it has been used by the United Reformed Church. Near the top of Cheviot Street and to your right is Wooler Youth Hostel. This is one of the numerous hostels offering comfortable accommodation to members of the Youth Hostel Association.

🌡 **The road curves left to a fork in the road as it leaves Wooler. Take the hedge-lined road to the right. It will be signposted for Earle and Middleton Hall. Continue until you see a rough track branching off to the right. The track will be signposted for the Pin Well and Waud House. Leave the road and turn down the track to arrive at a fork. Take the lesser path to the left that leads you through the trees and into a small valley. On coming to a gate set in a** stone wall, pass through and walk ahead for 200 metres to reach the spring known as the Pin Well.

The Pin Well is a small spring surrounded by a circle of rough stones. According to legend the well is the home of a fairy. It is said that anyone making a wish and dropping a bent pin into the water on May Day will have his or her wish granted before the end of the year. This practice appears to continue to this present day as bent pins can often be seen in the clear water. The custom is probably a relic of the well-worship practised in Pagan times.

↳ After passing the well, the path bends to the right below a promontory of rock.

This projecting piece of porphyry is known as the King's Chair. Legend tells of an ancient king who sat upon this rock to direct a mighty battle being fought below him. Behind King's Chair is a prehistoric site known as Kettles Camp. This covers an area of about 1¼ hectares (3 acres), and contains some fine examples of earthworks and entrenchments.

↳ The path continues up the valley then divides. Take the path to the right, which takes you along the base of a gorse-clad hillside. There will be a

The King's Chair

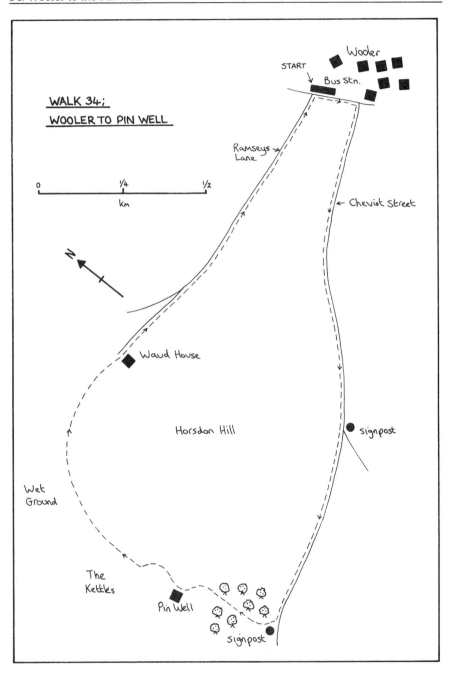

WALK 34;
WOOLER TO PIN WELL

Wooler

START

Bus Stn.

Ramseys Lane

← Cheviot Street

0   ¼   ½
km

N

Waud House

Horsdon Hill

● Signpost

Wet Ground

The Kettles

Pin Well

● signpost

fenced off area of wet land to your left. On reaching a gate set in a stone wall, pass through the gate. To your immediate right is red-roofed Waud House.

Waud House, or Wadhouse as it was originally named, was built in 1772. It stands on the western slope of Horsdean Hill. The hill was the site of an annual sheep and cattle market prior to the building of a permanent market in Wooler.

↳ Once through the gate, turn half-left to follow a rough stone road which curves around the front of Waud House. Wooler gradually becomes visible ahead of you. On reaching a surfaced road, turn right and follow the road as it descends into Wooler to arrive back at your starting point.

Local Attractions

Earle Mill Museum is 1¼ miles (2km) south of Wooler. This private museum is housed in an old granary building. It contains a fine and varied collection of farming and household antiquaries, including toys, kitchen equipment and farming tools. Enquiries and opening times, telephone 01668 281243.

35. ωOOLeℝ common cíℝcaℒaℝ

Distance: 2½ miles, 4 km
Grade: Easy
Maps: Ordnance Survey Landranger 75, Pathfinder 475 NT82/92
Refreshments: Wooler (1 mile) for numerous cafés, pubs and hotels.
Start: Wooler Common Nature Reserve car park. GR977273

Wooler Common is 1 mile west of Wooler, and reached by following Ramsay Street, opposite the bus station. Rothbury District of the Forestry Commission manages Wooler Common. An artificial lake has been created in the reserve. Around the perimeter of the lake a specially designed walkway for pushchairs, wheelchairs and the partially sighted has been installed. The lake is home to ducks, moorhens and wild fowl. Placed around the reserve are interpretative panels giving details of various animals and insects found in the reserve. Some of the trees have descriptive panels attached giving details about the species. This walk takes you around the reserve and provides excellent views of Wooler and the surrounding countryside.

↳ From the car parking area, cross the small footbridge to the left of the large notice board. The bridge spans the Humbleton Burn. A dirt path takes you along the edge of a mixed plantation. At the break in the trees to your left, leave the path and turn left up a broad path which steeply climbs through trees to a gate set in a stone wall.

To the right of the gate is a thoughtfully placed wooden seat. I have often sat there recovering from the climb. In my younger days it was nothing, but today is another matter!

↳ Go through the gate and straight ahead on a grassy path that ascends a gentle rise.

In summer the path is lined with bracken that changes to a rich brown in autumn.

↳ At the crest of the rise the path curves left to a gate in a wire fence. Pass through the gate and turn immediately left to pass through another gate. A few paces on is a small wooden marker post. Turn left, as indicated by a yellow arrow, to climb a gentle slope with a wire fence to your left. Pass by a stile.

At this point it is well worth crossing the stile and heading to a small cairn and stone wall visible ahead. From the cairn the view overlooking Wooler and the surrounding countryside is exceptional. Return to the stile and recross the fence to continue.

↳ After passing the stile, walk on to reach a gate set in a stone wall. Go through the gate.

To the left of the gate is a wooden seat, ideal for a brief rest and to admire the view of the valley below. The Cheviot Hills line the skyline to the south and east.

↳ Turn half-right to slowly descend to the valley floor. On the way down you pass through gorse bushes, a sulphurous yellow and fragrant when in bloom. At the foot of the descent, go through a gate to your left and on to a narrow,

Looking west from the summit of Brown's Law with Cheviot in the background

surfaced road. Turn left down the road.

Below to your right flows Humbleton Burn. The road is particularly narrow so beware of oncoming cars. The road runs from the nature reserve to Commonburn House and, except for access, is only partially open.

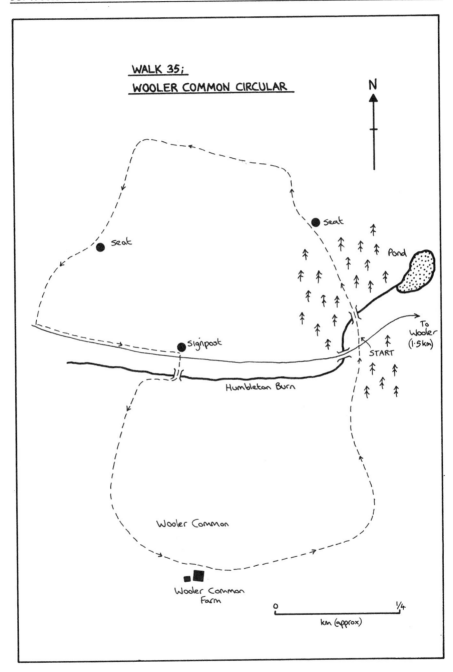

↳ Some 800 metres down the road you will encounter a signpost on your right bearing directions to Broadstruther.

At this point those wishing to cut short the walk should continue down the road to return to the starting point.

↳ Otherwise, turn right at the signpost and go down a slight slope to cross a wooden footbridge spanning Humbleton Burn. After a dozen paces pass through a gate and cross a narrow stream. Turn half right across pastureland to a dilapidated stone wall. At the wall, turn left on a broad path and keep the stone wall to your right. On coming to a fork, take the left fork. A narrow path climbs a short rise and takes you across rough pasture.

You are crossing Wooler Common. The local people of Wooler had grazing rights on this land until 1867 when nine freeholders were granted allotments of 0.5 hectares.

↳ Pass to the left of Wooler Common Farm to a signpost. Turn left and down a broad track to a marker post. Again turn left, following a lesser path that descends gently to a gate. Cross a stile next to the gate to return to your starting point.

36. Wooler Common to Commonburn

Distance: 7 miles, 11.4km

Grade: Medium

Maps: Ordnance Survey Landranger 75, Pathfinder 475 NT82/92, Outdoor Leisure 16

Refreshments: Cafés, pubs and hotels in Wooler (1 mile)

Start: Wooler Common nature reserve car park. GR 977273

An enjoyable excursion into the lower foothills of the Cheviots, travelling through forests and across moor. A walk along Hell Path provides a stimulating end to the walk.

 From the car park, continue up the narrow, surfaced road to cross a small bridge spanning the Humbleton Burn. Keep to the road and pass the house of Petersfield. After 500 metres the road deteriorates and climbs to pass along the side of a coniferous plantation on your right. Keep to the road for a further 200 metres to go along the side of another plantation.

Looking across the valley to your right you will see a number of gullies and large furrows on the opposite side. This area is known as The Trows. These features were formed at the end of the last Ice Age. Meltwater from the retreating glaciers carved these channels under hydrostatic pressure.

 The road enters a plantation and takes you through trees before exiting the other side on to moorland. A further 900 metres brings you to the buildings of Commonburn House. Turn left at the farm and descend a short slope to ford across the Common Burn.

Should fording the stream prove difficult, especially after heavy rain, there is a footbridge a short distance upstream.

 From the burn, a grassy path leads to a stile. Cross the stile and bear right to the next stile. Once over this one turn half right across rough moorland to a plantation. A stile allows you to enter the trees. Follow a path through the trees to another stile, which allows you to leave the plantation.

Throughout the Cheviots there are large plantations of coniferous trees. After the First World War the country found itself desperately short of timber. The Forestry Commission was established with the aim of reforesting the country and providing a reserve stock of timber for future needs.

↳ Follow a path which gently climbs the slope of a hill. Once over the top the path descends. Marker posts guide you along. On coming to the post at the foot of the hill, turn left as directed, to a gate.

The ruined buildings seen ahead as you descend are those of Broadstruther Farm. The last occupant was killed in a great storm after the Second World War. Since then the farm has been abandoned and left to decay.

↳ Pass through the gate and cross moorland. Pass through a stretch of gorse bushes and broom before going through an area of newly planted broad-leaved trees. The path drops to a wooden footbridge spanning the Common Burn.

The area is rich in ground nesting birds and walkers should keep to the right of way. If you have a dog with you, please make sure it is on a lead.

↳ Cross the bridge and turn right along the bank of the burn. Just after the point where the Common Burn is joined by another burn coming in from the right, pass through a gate in the fence to your left. Turn right and climb a broad path through trees. This is Hell Path.

The name Hell Path is probably a corruption of hill path. In season the sides of the path are adorned with foxglove and bracken. Pharmacists used to extract a drug used to treat certain forms of heart disease from the leaves of the foxglove plant. Its chemical name was digitalis and it slowed down the heart rate, reversing dangerous tachycardia. Today the drug is artificially produced in a purer form.

↳ At the top of the climb pass through a gate. A path leads you across rough grass to another gate. Pass through and on to yet another gate. Once through this one the path runs along the side of a plantation.

Looking ahead there are fine views overlooking the Northumbrian countryside to the east. On clear days the North Sea is visible beyond the distant hills.

↳ The path descends to follow an old stone wall. Pass through the gate when you reach it and turn left to go along the side of Wooler Common Farm. The path joins a broad track and leads to a gate.

Part of the next section travels along part of St Cuthbert's Way. This is a long distance footpath of 100km stretching from Melrose in Scotland to Holy Island off the Northumbrian coast.

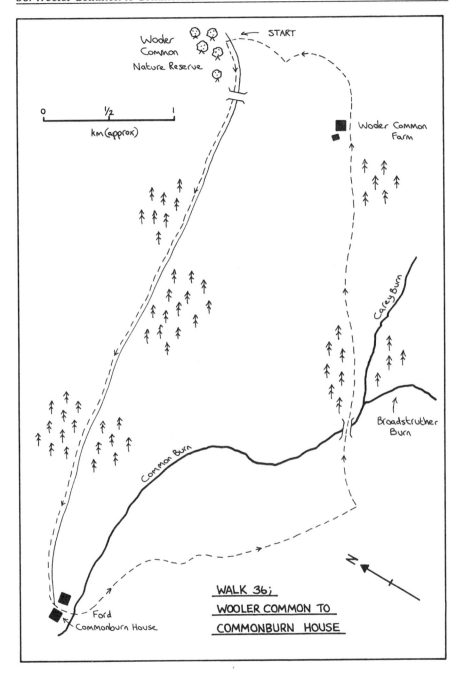

Wooler Common Nature Reserve

START

Wooler Common Farm

0   ½   1
km (approx)

Carey Burn

Broadstruther Burn

Common Burn

Ford
Commonburn House

N

WALK 36;
WOOLER COMMON TO
COMMONBURN HOUSE

Cheviot goats

↳ Go through the gate and keep a stone wall to your right. Pass a signpost for Broadstruther and walk on to a marker post. Turn left and follow a path, which descends to a stile. Cross the stile and go along a grassy path to return to your starting point.

During a summer walk I was delighted to see two red squirrels chasing each other across the stile. I watched for quite a while as they scampered backwards and forwards before dashing off into the trees.

37. ᴡooleʀ common to gleaᴏscleᴜgh

Distance: 7 miles, 11.2km

Grade: Strenuous

Maps: Ordnance Survey Landranger 75, Pathfinder 475 NT82/92, Outdoor Leisure 16

Refreshments: Wooler (1 mile) has cafés, pubs and hotels.

Start: Wooler Common car park. GR977273

On this walk you are almost certain to see grouse, and if you are lucky you may see deer as you cross the moors. A good portion of this walk follows St Cuthbert's Way, a recently-established long distance footpath between Melrose and Holy Island. The views on this walk are special and memorable.

✤ Go to the left of the information board and cross the bridge spanning the Humbleton Burn. After 50 metres reach a marker post bearing a St Cuthbert's Way emblem, a cross inside a circle. Turn left to climb a broad path rising steeply between trees to a gate at the top. Pass through the gate and go ahead on a broad grassy path up a slope. At the crest the path bends left and leads to a gate.

During the latter part of this section there are many fine views to the east, overlooking Wooler and the surrounding countryside.

✤ Go through the gate and sharp left through another gate. A few metres on is a marker post. Turn right up a bracken-lined path. At the top of the rise the path bends right, parallel to a wire fence. Where the fence turns right, keep to the main path and ignore a lesser path to the right. The path climbs and contours around the hill.

As you circle the hill there are good views to the right overlooking the Milfield Plain.

✤ Remain on the path with a stone wall to your right. On coming to a gate set in a stone wall, go through the gate.

To the side of the gate is a notice asking you to take care because of ground nesting birds and to keep dogs on leads.

✤ Follow a broad path through heather, resplendent in late summer, to cross grouse moor. Pass by a marker post bearing a St Cuthbert's Way emblem. The path rise towards Gains Law and curves left to pass below the summit.

Looking ahead you can see Yeavering Bell. The summit of the hill is crowned with the remains of an ancient hill fort.

↳ The path descends to a wire fence and bends left. At a marker post, turn half left to a wire fence crossed by a stile. Once over the stile, turn left. A dozen paces on the path forks. Take the fork to the right and climb a slope. After crossing an open expanse of moor the path comes to the corner of a stone wall. Walk on, keeping the stone wall to your right.

As you cross the moor you may come upon little piles of quartz grit. These have been laid down for the benefit of the game birds that inhabit the moor. The grit aids the birds digestion in breaking up the heather which it feeds on.

↳ On reaching a gate in the wall, leave the path and go through. Walk on with the stone wall to your left to a wire fence. Cross the stile and continue on with the wall still to your left.

As you walk you will notice wooden structures on the moor to your right. These are shooting butts.

↳ At a marker post turn right and angle away from the wall. Pass a large stone cairn to the right of the path. At the next marker post turn right along a stone track. After 40 metres go through a gate and along the side of a plantation on your right. The track bends right to go through a gate and down the other side of the trees. Keep to the track and pass to the right of a small plantation surrounded by a wire fence and a stone wall. At a wire fence across the way, go through the gate. Continue down the rim of the valley of the Akeld Burn and through the next gate.

The house ahead is the shepherd's house at Goldscleugh. Once abandoned and empty, it has been renovated and is now privately owned.

↳ After the gate the track bends right to cross the Akeld Burn. Walk on to a gate but do not go through. Turn right and go up the slope with a stone wall to your left. On coming to the end of the wall there will be a gate to the left, which you go through. Follow a path which runs parallel to a stone wall before bending right and climbing the slope of Harehope Hill. The path then contours the hill to a gate in a stone wall.

The views to the left as you circle the hill are tremendous. Excellent views overlooking the Milfield Plain delight the eye. To the far north the view encompasses Scotland.

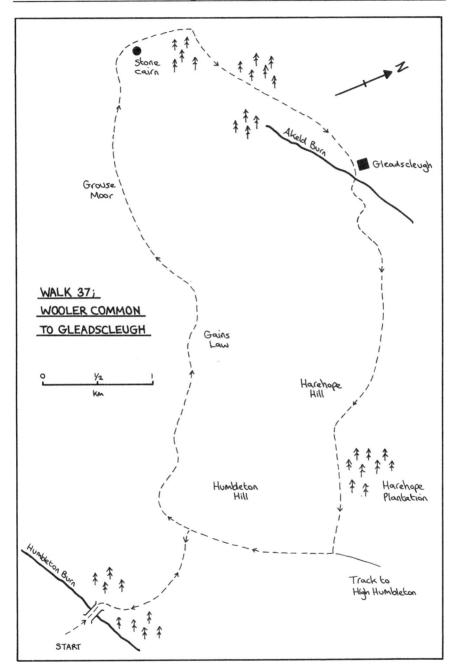

WALK 37;
WOOLER COMMON
TO GLEADSCLEUGH

0   ½   1
         km

Stone
cairn

Grouse
Moor

Akeld Burn

Gleadscleugh

Gains
Law

Harehope
Hill

Humbleton
Hill

Harehope
Plantation

Humbleton Burn

Track to
High Humbleton

START

Overlooking the nature reserve at Wooler Common

⅍ Cross the wall via a ladder stile next to the gate. Descend a steep slope to another gate in a stone wall. Cross, using a ladder stile. The path climbs slightly before travelling around the base of Humbleton Hill to a gate.

Humbleton Hill has a massive, prehistoric hill fort on the summit. The hill is also famous as it was here in 1402 that an English army under the command of Henry Percy defeated a Scottish army led by Archibald, Earl of Douglas. The Scots were utterly routed and fought their way past Akeld to the safety of Scotland. Some 500 of them drowned crossing the River Tweed.

⅍ Pass through the gate and through bracken, keeping next to a stone wall. At a marker post turn left. Further marker posts guide you along until you reach a gate. Pass through this gate and the next one to a farm track. Turn right and climb the track to a gate. Do not go through this gate. Look left and you will see another gate, go through this one. A grassy path leads through bracken before bending right and descending to a gate. Pass through the gate and descend through the trees to return to your starting point.

More books for the North-East from:

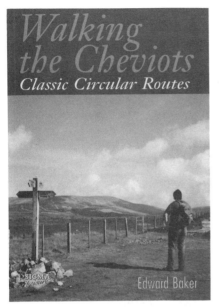

WALKING THE CHEVIOTS: Classic Circular Routes

This book, also by Edward Baker, is one of the few guides to the Cheviots. It includes nearly 50 walks, from 2 to 14 miles. "This book is a must for the Cheviot walker, whether experienced in the area or a visitor eager to explore this unique range of northern hills" - RAMBLING TODAY. £7.95

NORTHUMBRIA WALKS WITH CHILDREN

Covering the North East from the Tees to the Tweed, this guide book by local author Stephen Rickerby includes over 20 walks suitable for families. There are questions and spotting checklists to interest the children, as well as practical information for parents. All less than 5 miles long, the walks explore the great variety of scenery and heritage of Northumbria. As the parent of a young child himself, the author knows how to make sure children don't get bored! £6.95